MIRROR MIRROR

Dedicated to the memory of Felix Partz and Jorge Zontal.

This catalogue accompanies the exhibition
AA Bronson: Mirror Mirror
organized by the MIT List Visual Arts Center, presented
February 7–March 31, 2002.

Support for this exhibition has been provided by the
Canadian Department of Foreign Affairs and International Trade,
University Park Hotel at MIT, the Canadian Consulate General
in Boston, and Circa50.com.

The MIT List Visual Arts Center and its programs are generously
supported by the Institute of Museum and Library Services,
the Massachusetts Cultural Council, and the Council for the Arts
at MIT.

MIT List Visual Arts Center
Wiesner Building E15
20 Ames Street
Cambridge, MA 02139
(617) 253-4680
http://web.mit.edu/lvac

Design by Barr Gilmore

Printed in Canada by Bowne of Toronto

Available through D.A.P./Distributed Art Publishers
155 Sixth Avenue, 2nd Floor, New York, NY 10013
Tel. (212) 627-1999; Fax (212) 627-9484

ISBN 0-938437-63-1

AA Bronson thanks everyone at the MIT List Visual Arts Center
for this opportunity to shape an exhibition as the work evolved.
In particular, Jane Farver's rigor and Bill Arning's quicksilver
mind assured the success of the project. Special thanks to
Barr Gilmore and Mark Krayenhoff.

MIRROR MIRROR

AA BRONSON

Organized by Bill Arning, MIT List Visual Arts Center

It happened while I was sitting on the chair at the psychiatrist's. I say the chair, because he did not have me lie down: I sat up, abruptly upright usually, and gripped the arms of the chair as we talked. He had an innate knack for bringing me out of my head and into my body, usually with a few words. When it happened it was without warning: the sense of the looking glass straight in front of me, almost pressed to my face, a warm and foggy mirror, a mirror colored by steam, a membrane to another world. On the other side I could see someone moving, a vague shape of flesh, the sense of terror. My blood ran cold, I gripped the arms of my chair, the hairs on the nape of my neck stood straight up, prickling, I froze, and then burst into tears. I have never revisited this moment; I keep waiting for it to reappear, but it has not.

I first saw this mirror in the late eighties, hanging on a column in Mokotoff Fine Arts on the fourth floor of a building across the street from the New Museum on Broadway in New York City. It had a smoky mysterious quality, and I was immediately drawn to it. Moke told me that it was smuggled out of Tibet in order to raise money for a monastery, and that it was a seventeenth or eighteenth century divination mirror used by the State Oracle of Tibet. My understanding is that each oracle in turn is given his own mirror; as in many Asian cultures, the Tibetans place no particular value on old things. It is the spiritual practice within which the mirror plays its role that is important: the mirror is a prop on the material plane. It has no inherent value or significance.

When advising the Dalai Lama, the State Oracle wears an elaborate costume, including this mirror on his chest. In deep trance, he looks into the mirror, not directly, but through another mirror held by an assistant in front of him. Through this doubly distant vision he foretells the future and gives advice.

When Jorge and I went to Dharamsala in 1982 to photograph the Dalai Lama, we found ourselves waiting some ten days for him to return, late, from a journey. One of many events that befell us was dinner with the State Oracle, an elderly man in his seventies. The State Oracle, whose name I have never remembered, had eyes unlike any I had seen before. It was as if his head was hollow, and fire was burning deep within the sockets. The expression "he looked right through me" is not adequate here. They were the eyes, I believe, of one who has undergone intense purification. Possibly they were also the eyes of the spirit that inhabited him.

Back in New York, I returned to look at the mirror many times. I could not afford to buy it.

Some years later, the Gagosian Gallery held a fund-raising exhibition to benefit Tibet House in New York. The exhibition consisted of major works by contemporary artists, but also included my precious mirror. This came at a time when I had money in my pocket, and although the price was now dramatically increased, I purchased the mirror. I wrapped it in a dark blue shawl, and I kept it hidden, as if its power would be diminished by exposing it to view.

It was only while working on the current exhibition that the relationship of this mirror to my own work became apparent to me, most directly to my mirror self-portraits of 1969.

I had hidden the mirror from life, during a period in which I was preoccupied with death. But now I expose it to light again, to allow myself to see into its smoky realm of possibilities.

Tibetan, 17th Century
Attributed as the Mirror of the State Oracle of Tibet
"seven metal" silver alloy, gold, and turquoise
10-1/2 inches diameter

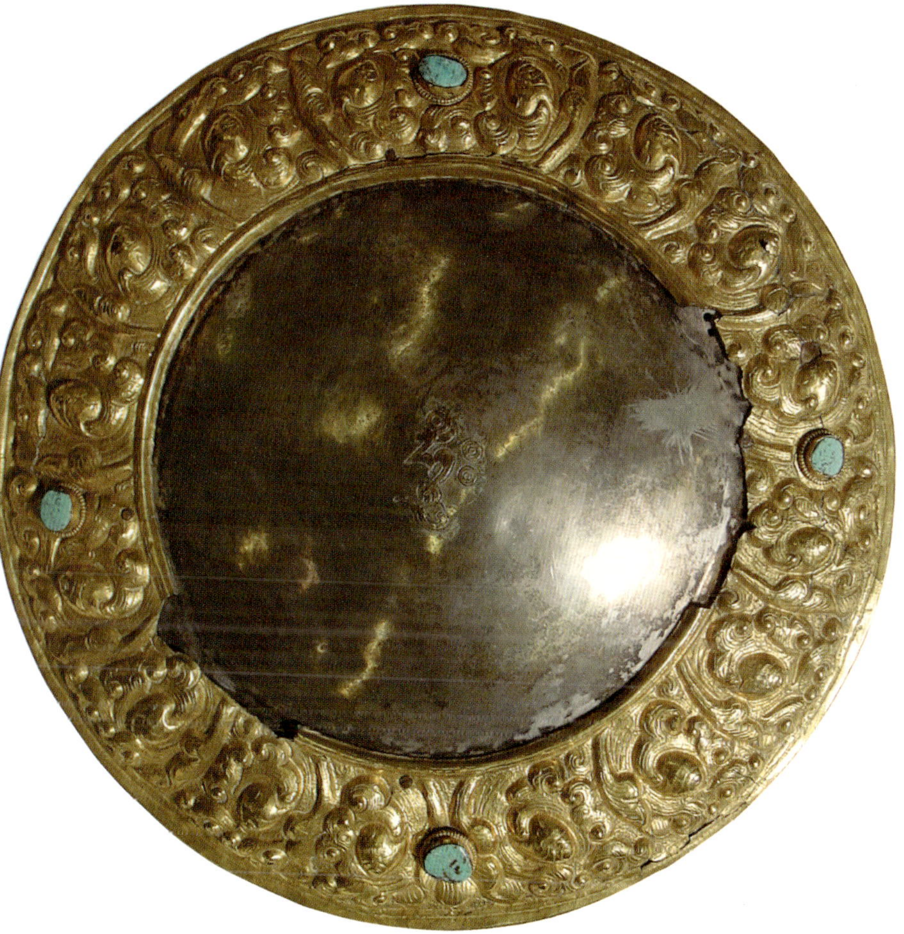

In 1968, when I began taking self-portraits, I was concerned with the body: more specifically, with my body, and with my body in relation to my friends' bodies. I had no other way to measure the world. Lacking an identity, or any way to judge my separation from others, I began with my physical self. This would later prove inadequate, but it was a beginning.

In the last few years, since the deaths of Felix and Jorge, my attention has returned to the body, to my body and to theirs, as the residue of what was.

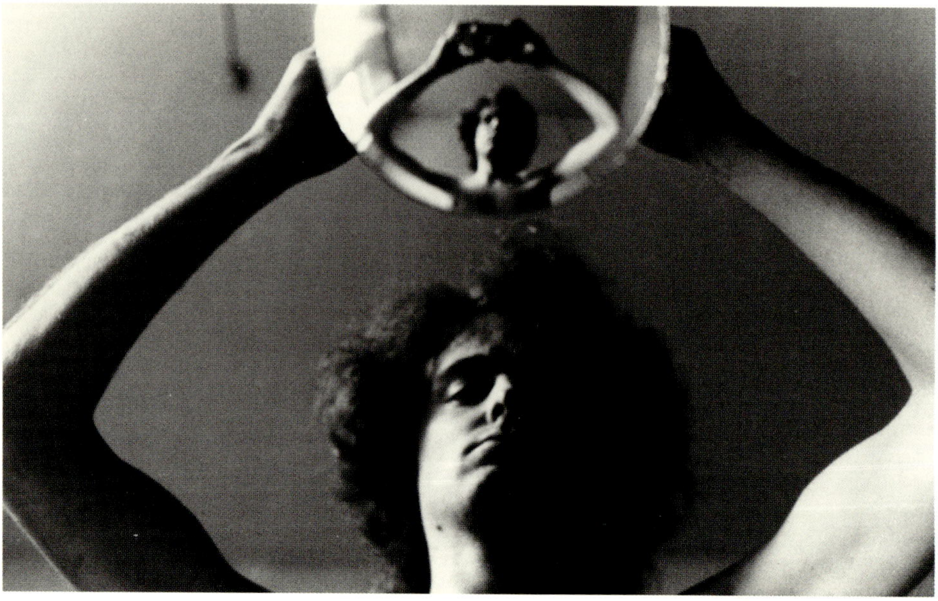

Mirror Sequences, 1969-70
seven vintage black-and-white photographs
six at 4-5/8 x 7-1/2 inches each, one 10 x 8 inches

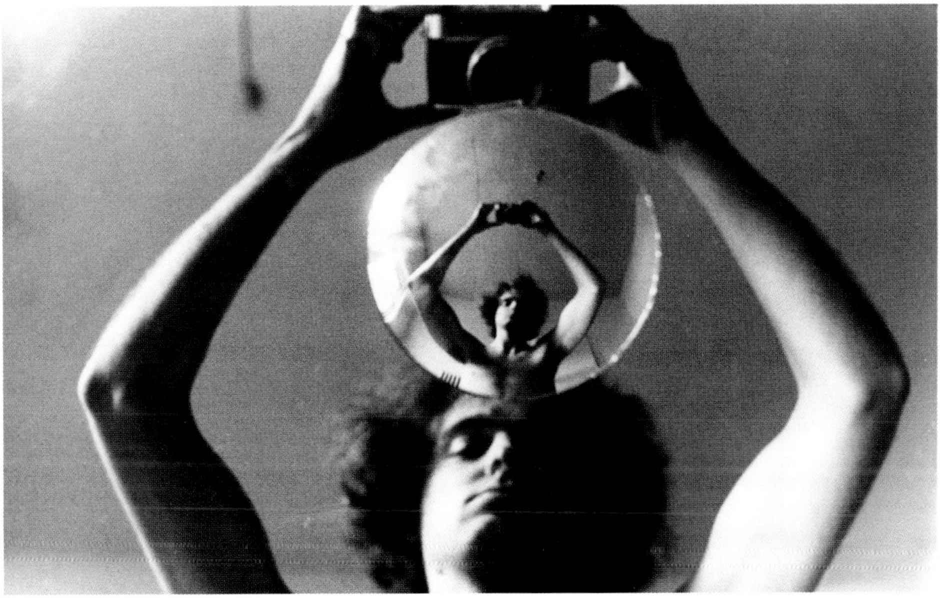

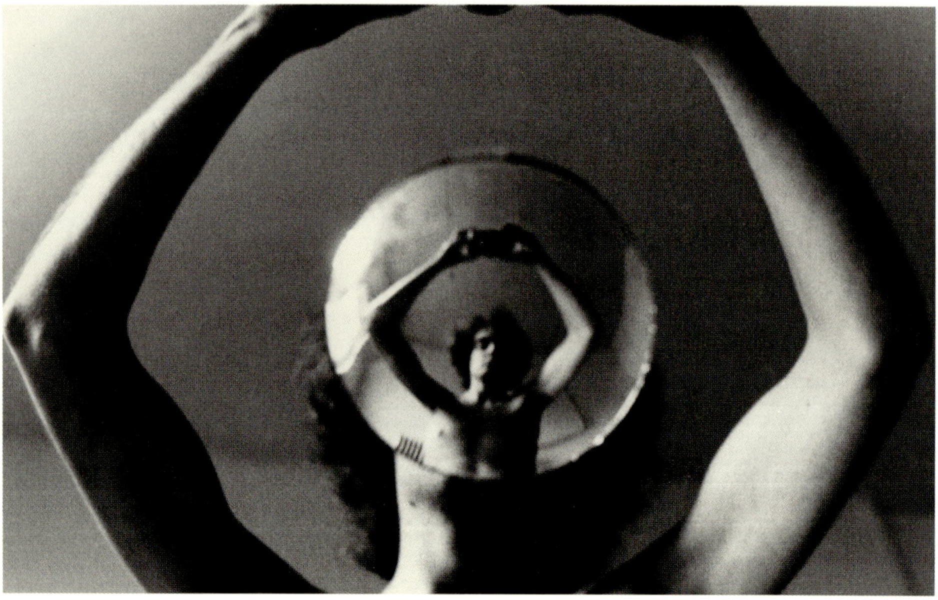

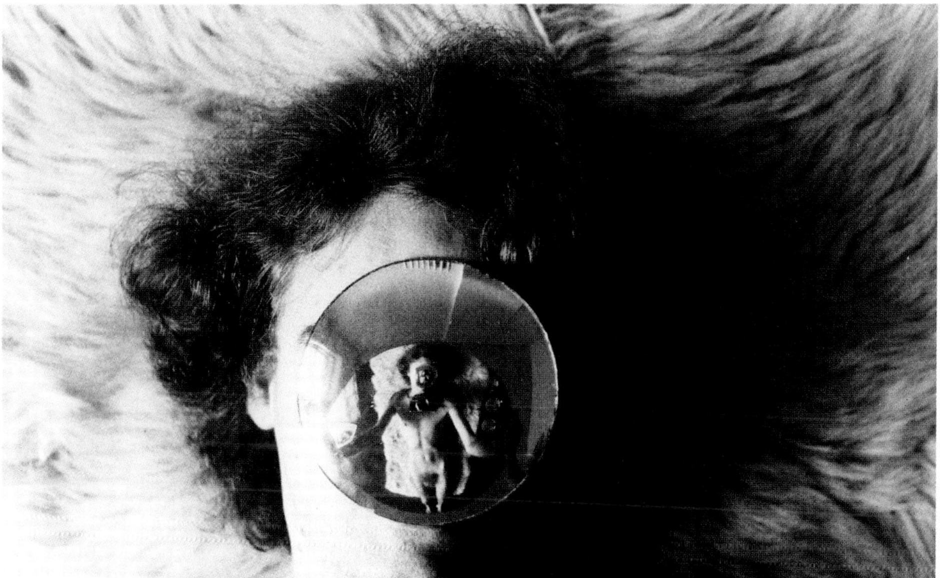

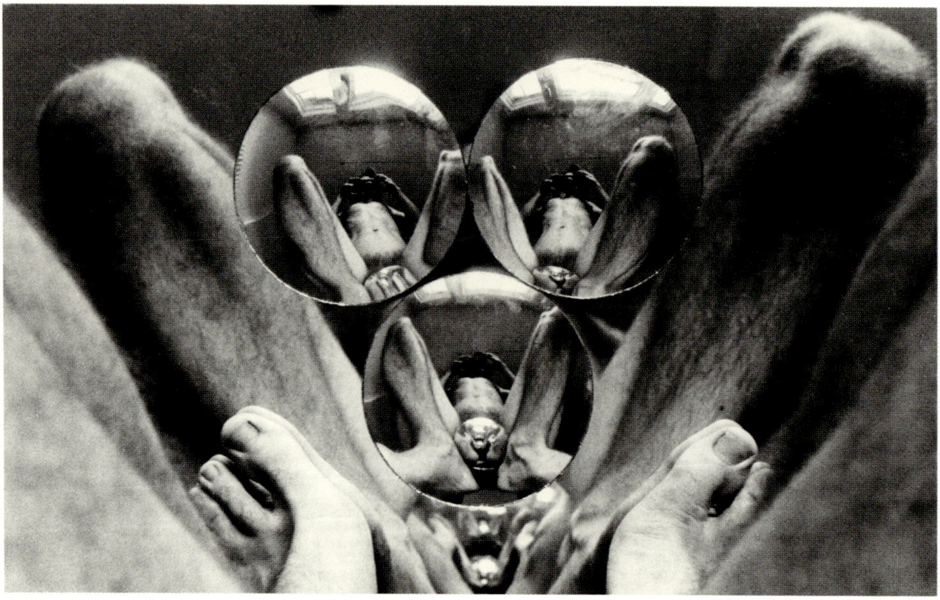

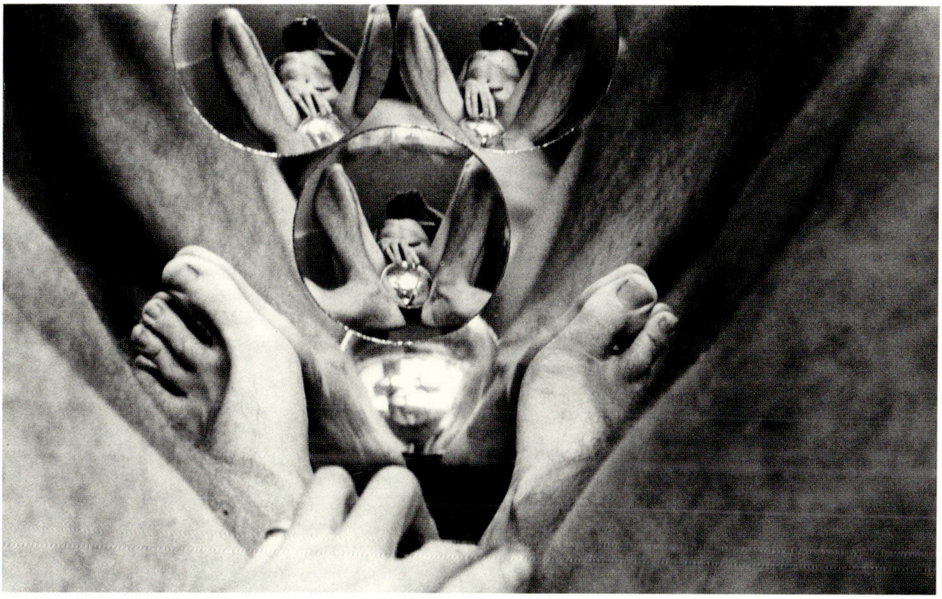

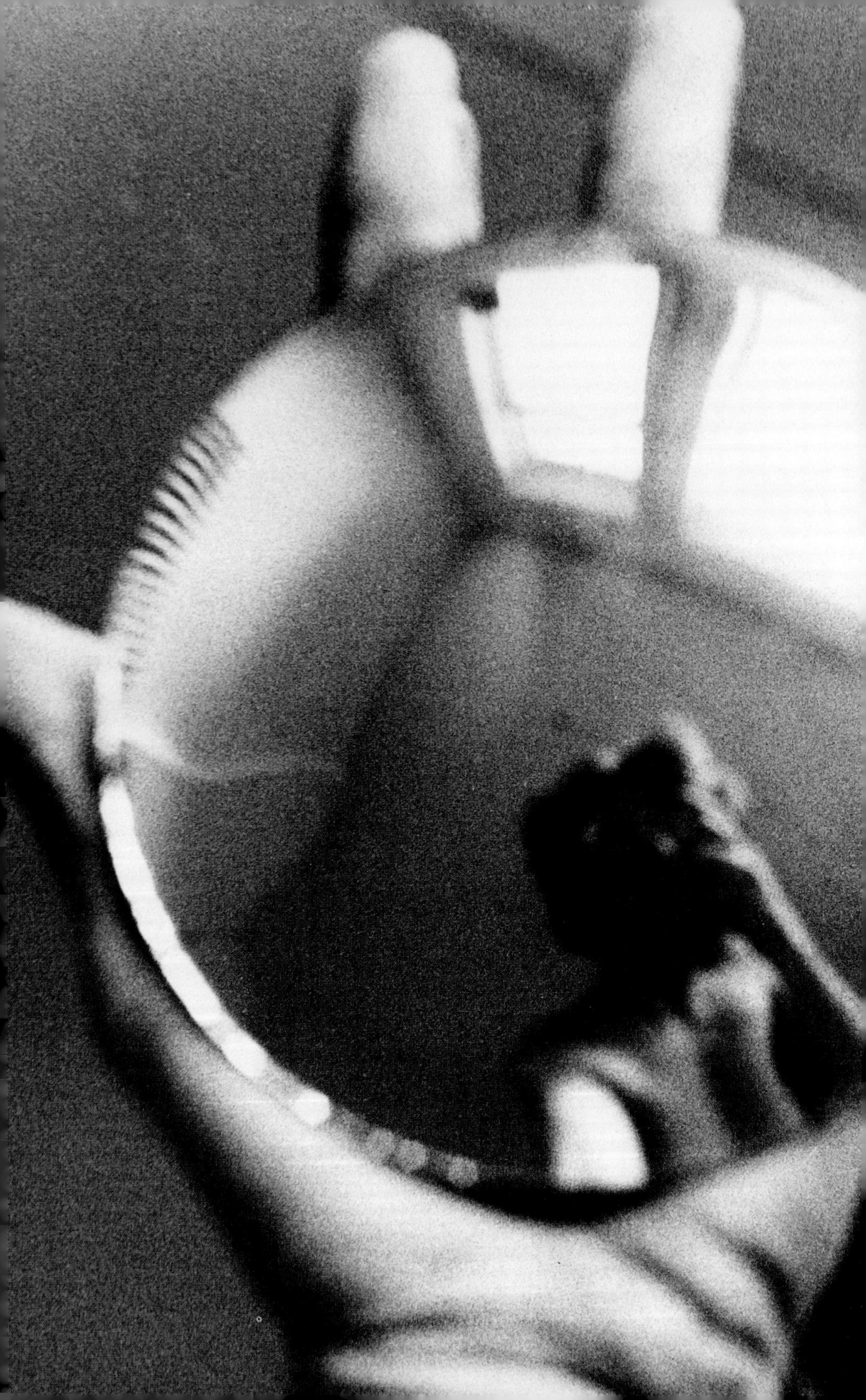

AA BRONSON'S MIRROR MIRROR

Bill Arning

AA Bronson's *Mirror Mirror* asks a simple question: "How do we live our lives and endeavor to create profound and lasting meanings against and through the great issues of our age?" This question originates from Bronson's singular biography, and that is of course merely one man's tale. However, these events, these personages, and these political, spiritual, and philosophical questions point toward a way of reconciling oneself with one's time, and with life on life's terms.

AA Bronson's unique life as he presents it to us has been consistently public and theatrical. As one of the three members of the artists' group General Idea for their 25-plus years of working and living together, Bronson employed his persona as the stuff of art. In 1994, their collaboration in art and life ended when Bronson's partners, Felix Partz and Jorge Zontal, died of AIDS-related causes, and Bronson faced the daunting task of resuming life as just AA Bronson.

While tragic, this is a universal experience, and the process of rejoining life after loved ones are lost is difficult to make newly vivid. But Bronson's case is unusual, as "AA Bronson" did not exist prior to General Idea. Rather, there was a young artist and architect named Michael Tims, who was investigating avant-garde strategies for the free exchange of ideas, communal living, and ways to break down the boundaries between art and life.[1]

When Tims met his future life-mates and joined with them to form General Idea, the group gradually evolved into a collective exploring media mythologies, for which he invented and came to inhabit the persona of AA Bronson. Through complex and wildly convoluted performance/installation events, they brought their three fictional self-creations of Bronson, Partz, and Zontal to life.

The members of General Idea were constantly obfuscating, mythologizing, and playing with fixed notions of the real. Historians have noticed that the first *Miss General Idea Pageants* supposedly occurred in 1968, while General Idea was not a named, functional entity until 1970.[2] This willful falsification was in the spirit of the group's McLuhanesque investigation of the media and General Idea's ethos was, "If it is written in a magazine, that makes it true, or at least as true as anything else."

General Idea's play with a constructionist idea of self in the early '70s seems prescient. Yet a simple household object—the mirror—fulfilled many of their goals. Mirrors are mesmerizing and seductive open metaphors, impermanent cameras, and devices for constituting self as well as examining selfhood. They became crucial to General Idea and occur frequently in Bronson's work today.

Tim Guest, art critic and a fellow traveler of General Idea wrote:

> *In the mirror's reflection you gaze into a psychological enigma at the same time as you recognize your public face. General Idea made extensive use of mirrors, "mirrors mirroring mirrors, mirroring mirrors.*[3]

One must be cautious, though, of seeing General Idea's use of mirrors as simply celebrating the world of surface appearances. While mirrors are the primal devices in which we see ourselves in this world and through which we learn of our existence as independent beings, and in which we fix our hair and make-up, they have another aspect crucial to Bronson's purposes. They are the tools through which we may begin to question the absolute reality of the world. The mirror-world presents an unreal, uninhabitable double of our world with a reality nearly as complete as ours. If that world can appear real, yet be an illusion, what does that imply about the one we seem to inhabit? Meditations on the mirror-world urge us to consider other models of understanding perceivable reality, and open the door to ever-expanding spiritual questioning.

AA Bronson's early works are represented in *Mirror Mirror* by the two series *Mirror Sequences* and *Body Binding*. These early series of works point toward the common experience of a young soul exploring the world through the vehicle of a sensate body. In *Mirror Sequences* circular convex mirrors reflect the body disassembled into distorted puzzle pieces that we may or may not be able to reconstitute as a coherent whole. In *Body Binding*, the bodily limits of self are reiterated: elastic digs into the artist's flesh as if diagramming its contours. It is as if the bound creature were asking incredulously, "Can this be it; can this be all I have in which to travel though the dangerous world?" It proved not to be. By joining General Idea, becoming AA Bronson, and becoming one of the preeminent drag queen/punk shamans of conceptual art, his body became much more than itself.

General Idea's work was often very funny, playing in the realm of fashion, coiffed poodles, metaphorical cocktails, mass culture, and celebrity. In the giddily intoxicated '70s, living in a world without dire consequences seemed possible, and one could live life as a manifestation of one's intellect and glamour. Tragedies happened, but they too could be played as theater. General Idea reveled in the mythical destruction of *The 1984 Miss General Idea Pavillion*.[4] Its smoldering ruins and remaining artifacts became the subjects of many of their exhibitions. History, even fabricated history, was the stuff of opera (soap or grand), mirroring the world while exaggerating its drama to better reveal its truths.

In the '80s, however, AIDS cut a cruel path through the landscape of the best and brightest cultural practitioners of the day, and any history of the period must include the diverse responses to the pandemic. General Idea's work in this field produced poetic and political masterpieces of our times, and General Idea is understandably best remembered today for their AIDS-related works, particularly in the U.S. where their earlier work was less widely exposed.[5] Their remake of Robert Indiana's *LOVE* icon as AIDS was a markedly simple gesture, reiterated in many different forms from posters to paintings to tabletop sculptures to an electronic billboard in Times Square. Along with Gran Fury's *Kissing Doesn't Kill*, ACT-UP's *Silence=Death* and Felix Gonzalez-Torres' *Untitled (Pillows)* billboard, this work has proven that political art does not necessarily have a short shelf life. It, like the others, has become a crucial part of our visual culture, and is taught in universities, available to future generations to reinterpret and use for their own strategies of resistance.

The AIDS pandemic, like the Holocaust before it, or terrorism since, has transformed our politics, passions, and souls altogether. Survivors of such tragedies cannot help but see every aspect of reality differently, and understand themselves within a continuum of common humanity and the unavoidable suffering inherent in being corporeal.

Bronson's response to personal trauma in *Mirror Mirror* is manifold, and begins, as all healing must, with the painful process of remembrance and with inventorying loss even when such truth telling is too painful to bear. Images of Felix and Jorge become visual records of their mortality, mirrored through the eyes of a beloved friend.

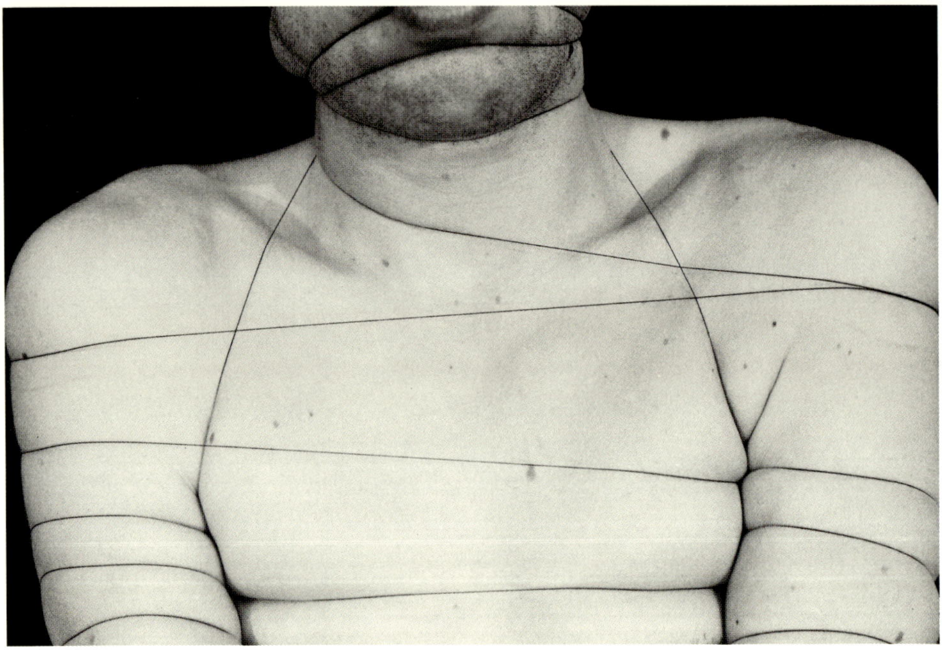

Body Binding, 1970
fifteen vintage black-and-white photographs (eight shown here),
assembled as an artist's book
5 x 7 inches each sheet
Art Metropole Collection, Library (Gift of Jay A. Smith, Toronto, 1999),
National Gallery of Canada, Ottawa

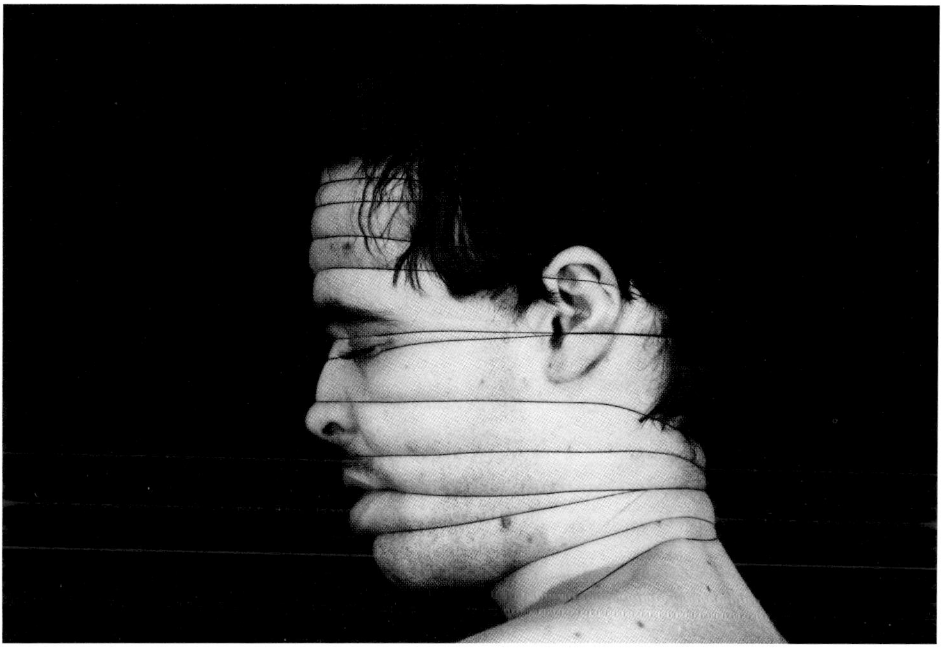

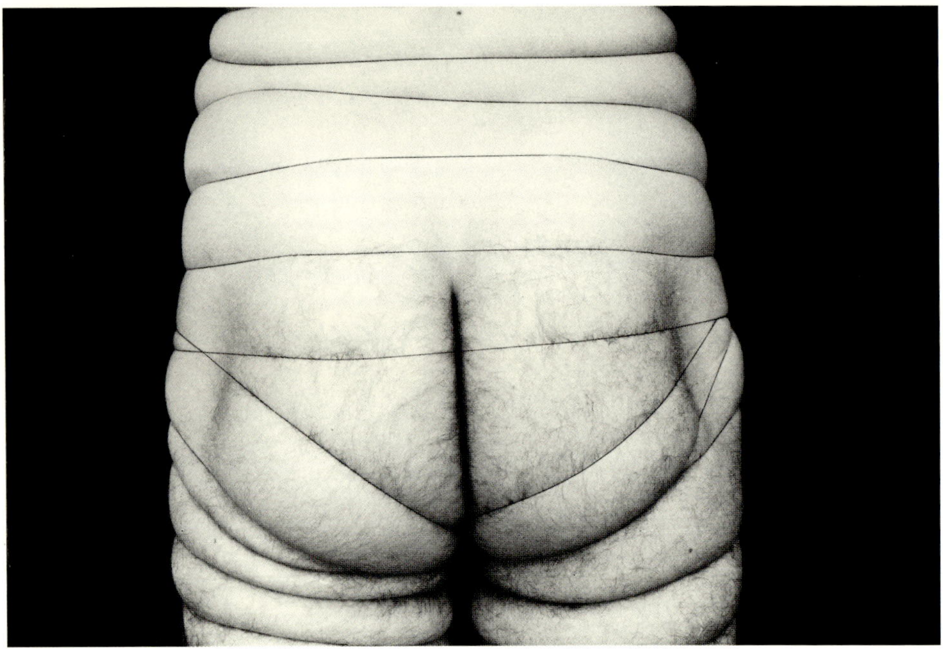

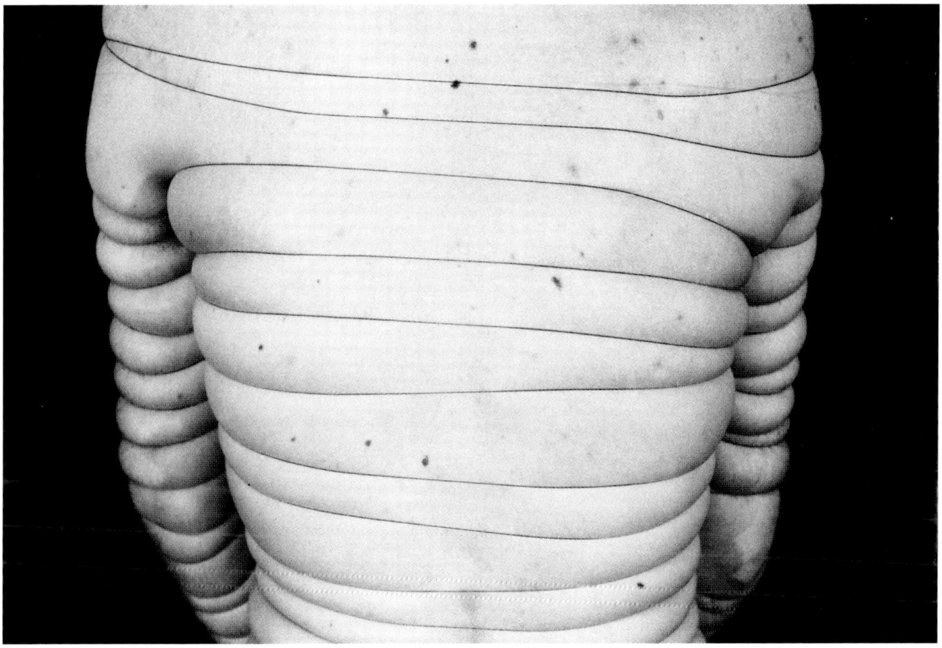

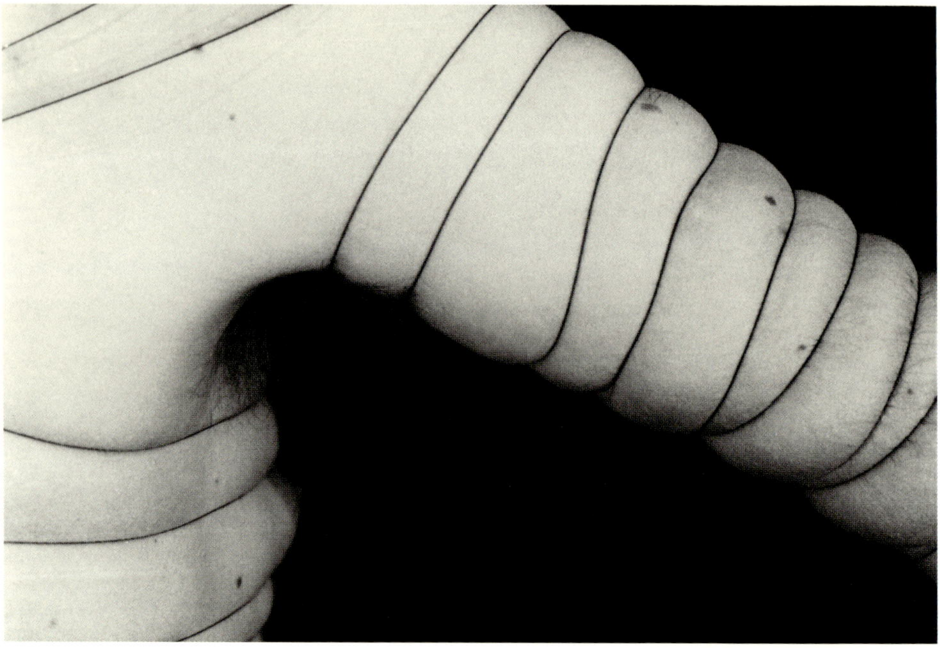

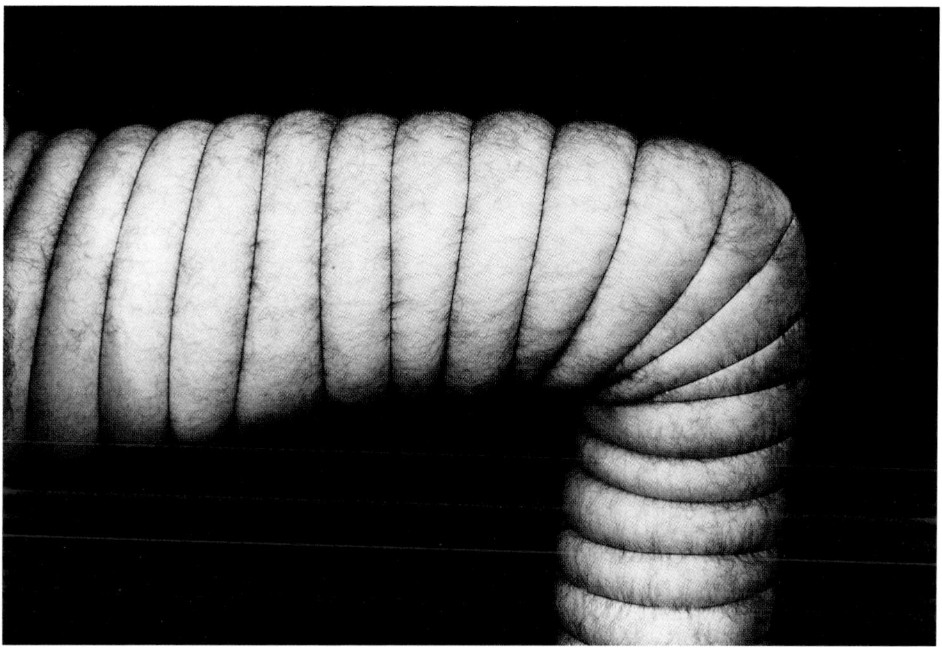

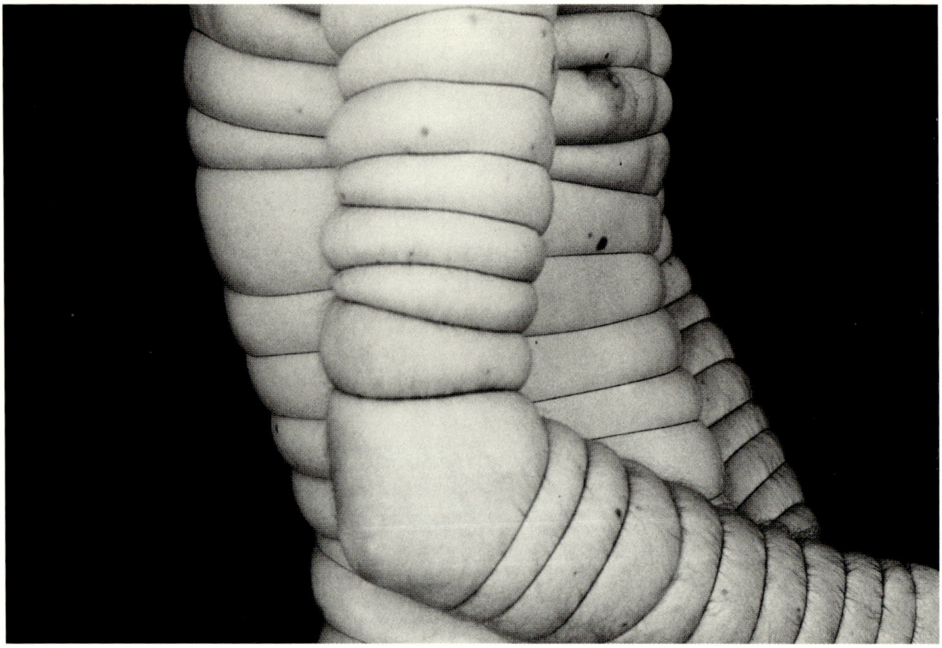

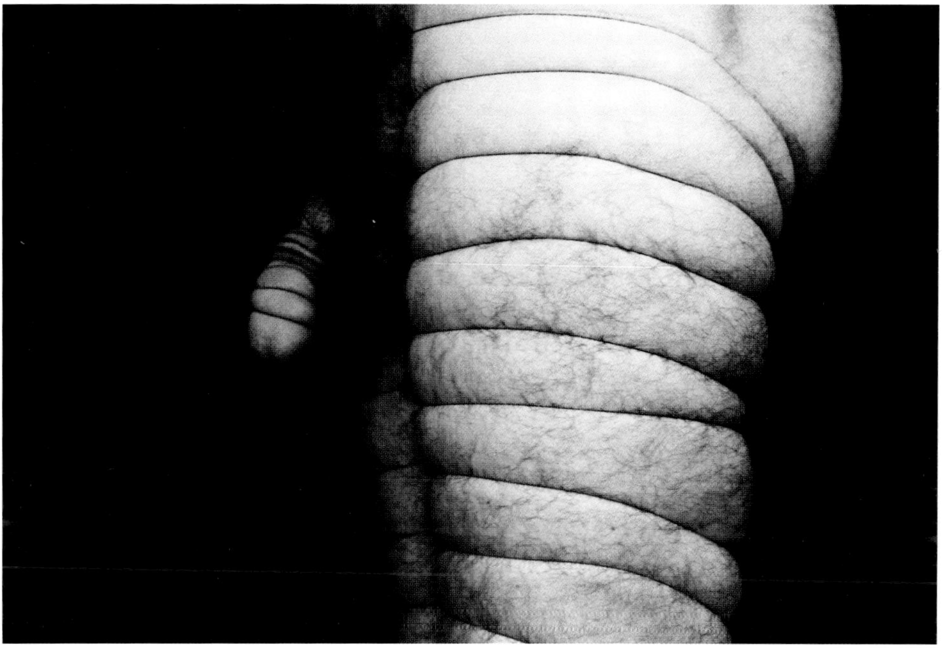

Although he was blind and could not see the resulting photographs, Jorge asked AA to document his emaciation as a link to his family history under the Nazis. *Jorge, February 3, 1994* speaks of the power of representations. Depiction makes the tragedy of suffering all too real in the world in which we must deal with suffering whether or not our best wishes, prayers, and actions prove futile. We must live our lives in the world of surfaces. Although that is not all there is to reality, it is the only world in which we can act directly—be it protesting government policies or caring for those who suffer.

The billboard-scale *Felix, June 5, 1994* is complex in its graphic depiction. Felix's face is so afflicted by wasting that even in death his eyes cannot close. Yet this is also an image of love. Felix is surrounded by evidence that he was cared for by those who loved him. The brightly colored fabrics swaddling Felix's body and his cigarettes and remote control still within reach tell of a man finding some joy in the small pleasures his friends could provide. That this photograph was taken at all testifies that there was a friend present at the end who wanted to remember his face—even when disease had made his visage strange and awful to those who did not know him.

Felix, June 5, 1994 exists in several versions, varying only in size. The smallest is a discrete, semi-private testament to one man's passing, a poetic marker of loss, while the largest speaks in the public language of advertising, and Felix's skeletal face becomes a public icon. As "Felix Partz," he stands in for countless others whose faces at death, whether from AIDS or some other form of tragedy, we are not privileged to know personally.

Felix Partz and Jorge Zontal are joined in *Mirror Mirror* by AA Bronson himself, naked and entombed in his self-portrait, *AA Bronson, August 22, 2000*. Many cultures make use of symbolic death rituals to mark rites of passage, but AA Bronson's symbolic death and rebirth is tantalizingly confusing in the realm of post-modernity: he is a mediated creation killed off with no more suffering than the cancellation of a television series.

Our standard way of thinking does not allow the cultural and the spiritual to mix. We may learn from Michel Foucault and the Dalai Lama, but we rarely integrate their lessons. It is as if their insights would by necessity contradict each other. But in Bronson's work such subversive ideas as an acceptance of impermanence and a questioning of the world of appearances, as well as any clear notion of selfhood, are derived equally from both thinkers' disciplines and are combined in startling harmony.

AA Bronson, August 22, 2000 is informed by the artist's recent *Hotel Series*: self-portraits photographed in hotel rooms while traveling, a metaphoric activity for our ongoing quest for meaning. We see the exposed body of a troubled and all-too-human being, recording his lack of identity. We look into the mirrors over the artist's shoulder and share his torment. He has the gift and curse of being alive and healthy, and his talent and mind are intact. What is not clear is what is the next right thing for him to do with that mind and talent. How do you endure a suffering so immense, take its lessons to heart, and move forward?

The bitter prescription in *Mirror Mirror* is in a field of convex mirrors that spells out "Arbeit Macht Frei," the slogan the Nazis raised over the portal of Auschwitz. This innocuous phrase, which echoes the North American work ethic, is today inseparable from murder; and seeing ourselves reflected hundreds of times in these words is in itself unbearable. We are often defined by our "work", whether that be a true calling, a vocation, or simply wage earning. To continue on that path after our world has been upended can lead to a profound soul sickness. One must struggle to be alive while one is alive. It is often said "Faith without works is dead"; and one may substitute the word "art" or "love" or even "life" for "faith," and the phrase remains true.

In 1999, Bronson returned to making art.[6] It is tempting to cheer and pretend all is well and his period of mourning is over. It is not. His art making today is the work of a haunted man trying to make sense of, and come to terms with, the unthinkable. His haunting is not pathological or pathetic; it is instead humbly human.

This exhibition is his third since his return to art. In each, his relationship to the past has changed. In this exhibition, we find the artist's willingness to lead us through the steps of the lessons he has learned. In Tibetan Buddhism all perceived reality is Karmic Theater, so that incarnations of our true selves can learn lessons and thereby move toward Nirvana. The life Bronson shares with us today is rich in lessons that he makes available to us in a spirit of generosity.

Bronson appears to be more a youthful gadfly than a grizzled teacher in these works. Still, he speaks of himself as old. The lessons of a rich life lived over time are rare in a youth obsessed world that is forever seeking its next Britney or N' Sync. Rarely do we hear the voices of those starting on second lives, outside of spiritual retreats.

AA Bronson's life today is represented by one large photo work. *Anna and Mark, February 3, 2001* represents Mark Krayenhoff, Bronson's spouse (referred to in Bronson's writing as the man who will lead him across the desert) holding Mark's 10-day-old daughter, Anna.[7] The politics of the image are immediate, giving rise to many complex feelings about alternative versions of the family, and the tenderness of this bearded masculine man holding a tiny infant. However, like a breaking wave, those simplistic reactions dissipate, leaving us grateful that we have bodies and are alive and sensate to share in the miracles of birth, life, and even death. Glancing from Felix's face at the end of his passage through this world, to Anna at the beginning of hers, we can only wonder what more there is to do than experience and share whatever joy and love is possible in this impermanent, finite, fragile existence? If we get a glimmer of greater wisdom, we are very lucky.

I have found no way to discuss this material in the distanced manner appropriate to a trained art historian. I am writing this paragraph on New Years Day, staring out into a frigid but beautiful Cambridge, Massachusetts, haunted by the losses of the past year. AA Bronson's *Mirror Mirror* is an inspiration for me in starting this new year. By the last days of the exhibition, spring will be in the air, and the promise of new life will be omnipresent. *Mirror Mirror* will help us cherish the time and the love we have.

1. See Fern Bayer, "The Search for the Spirit," *The Search for the Spirit: General Idea 1968-1975* (Toronto, Ontario: Art Gallery of Ontario, 1997), 10-12.
2. See Christina Ritchie,"Allusions, Omissions, Cover-Ups: The Early Days," *The Search for the Spirit: General Idea 1968-1975*, 13-16.
3. See Tim Guest, "From Ziggurats to Curlicues: A Few Principle Features in the Art of General Idea," *General Idea 1968-1984*, ed. General Idea and Jan Debbaut (Eindhoven: Stedelijk van Abbemuseum, 1984) 17-19.
4. See General Idea, "The 1984 Miss General Idea Pavilion," *General Idea 1968-1984*, 33-37. While the pavilion never existed, General Idea displayed photographs of themselves fleeing from the burning building, the rubble of the "Silver Bar," and replicas of the luxurious murals of copulating poodles that had supposedly adorned its walls. The Pavilion was the home of the *Miss General Idea Pageants*, some of which did happen in real life, and others only in the mythic realm of General Idea.
5. See Stephan Schmidt-Wulffen, "Between Faith and Hope: General Idea's PLA©EBO Series," *General Idea's Fin De Siècle*, ed. General Idea (Stuttgart, Württembergischer Kunstverein, 1992), 61-62.
6. The exception was one piece made in 1997, *Untitled (for General Idea)* in the form of three Bertoia chairs with custom vinyl cushions. As a portrait of the three members of GI, is best understood as a transitional piece in the most profound sense of the word, that of marking a significant life-changing event.
7. See AA Bronson, *Negative Thoughts* (Chicago: Museum of Contemporary Art, 2001), 84.

Hotel Photos, 1995-2000
five color c-prints
11 x 14 inches each

October 29, 2000

I dreamed I was in the bathroom in my Toronto apartment. The ceiling caved in over the bathtub in an explosion of soot and concrete. I looked out the bathroom door into a large space with no ceiling. Outside, explosions of soot and concrete lit up the night sky.
I remember asking myself if it was better to stay in the building for protection, or to leave in case it collapsed.

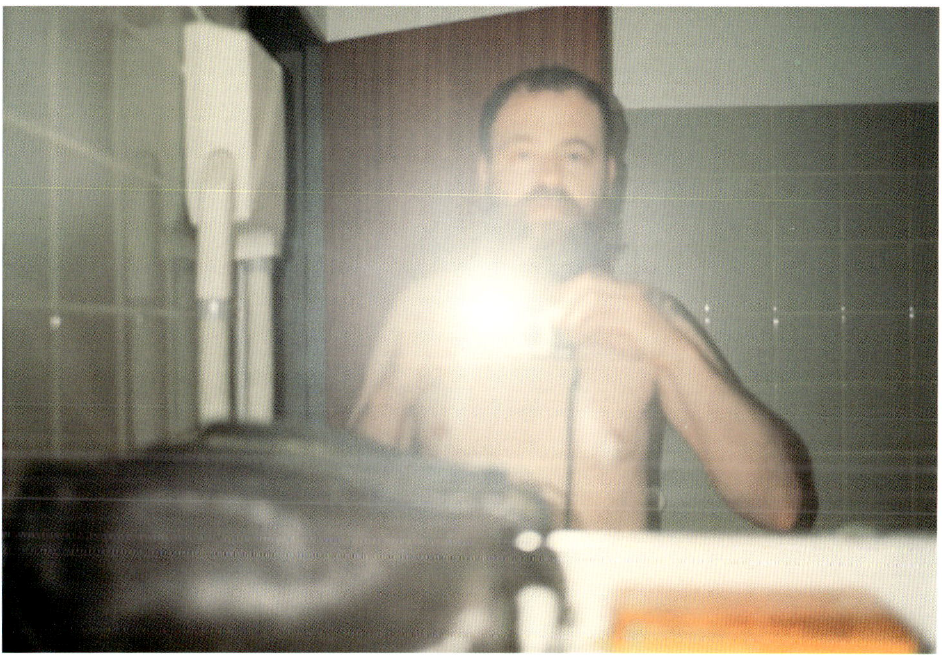

November 13, 2000

I dreamed of a fund-raising film in which a man with no lower torso or legs is rolling naked on the ground. No one wants to play with him because there is nothing you can do with him. He is like a big pink bowling ball with stick-like arms and a head. As we watch, he rolls down the slope of the sidewalk and comes to rest next to the tire of a bus.

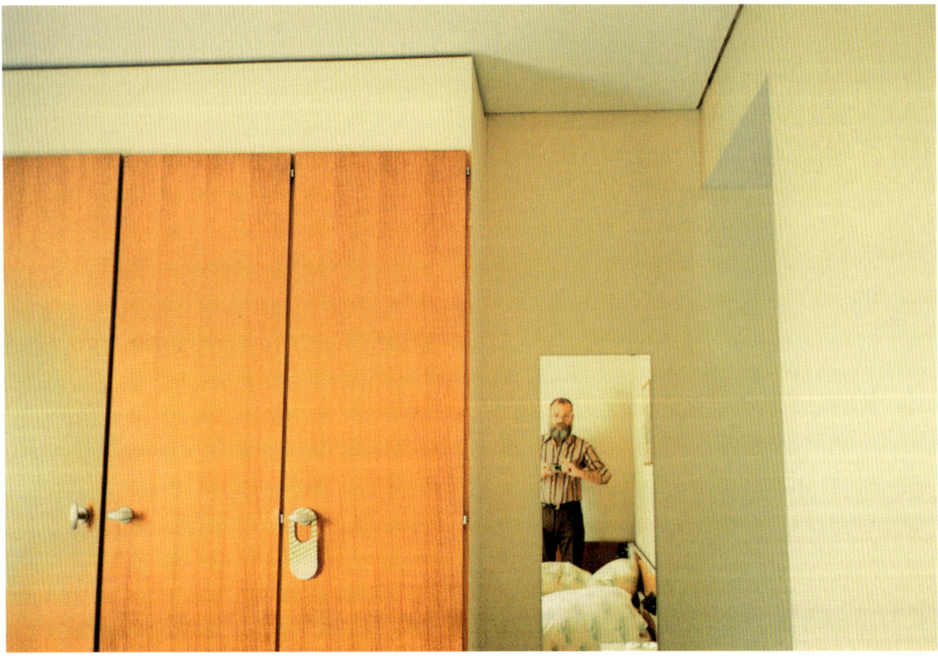

January 10, 2001

The night before last I dreamed that I committed suicide by drowning. I was with two men, one who might have been my father, another who might have been my son. We were standing waist deep in water, next to a row boat, similar to ones I went fishing in with my father when I was a child. My son tied a rope to my ankle, tying the other end to the back of a small boat, and I submerged down into the water until I was floating just above the bottom of the lake. I lay there quietly, watching, and wondering to myself if my life would flash before my eyes. It did not. I was aware that soon I would take a deep breath, and then I would drown. I felt very peaceful.
I wonder if this was a baptism.

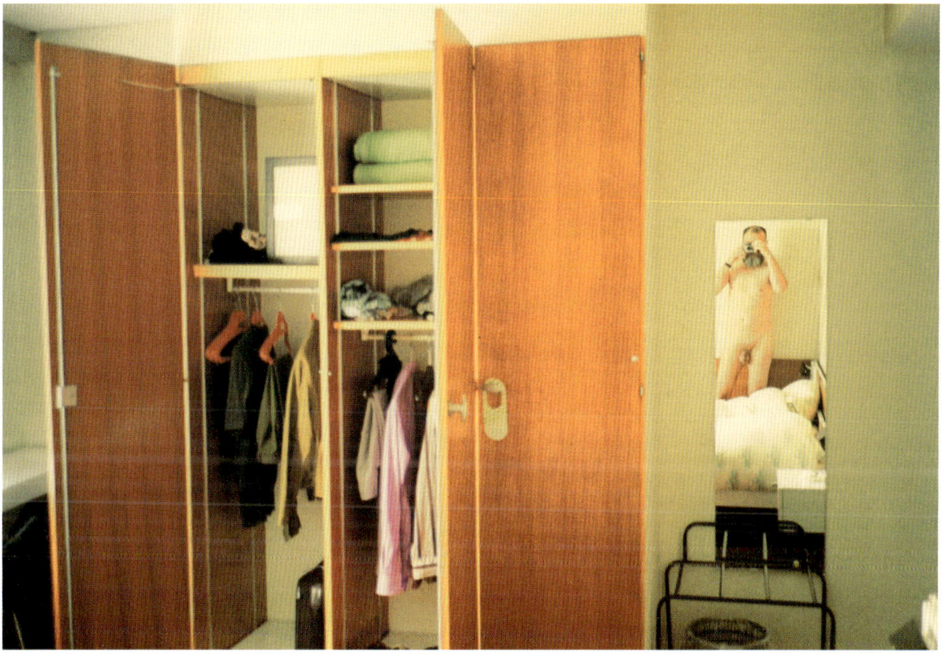

March 9, 2001

I dreamed that I was looking at a book with two words on the cover: Eloachim, and another that I do not remember. They were stamped in gold on a black leather or leatherette cover in quite large roman type. I had the sense that the meaning was something to do with angels. The dream felt very significant.

At lunch with Ealan, I asked him about the word. He said it was one of the synonyms for "God" or "Yaweh" in Hebrew, one of the names of God that may be spoken out loud. He said the spelling didn't matter, as it is transliteration anyway.

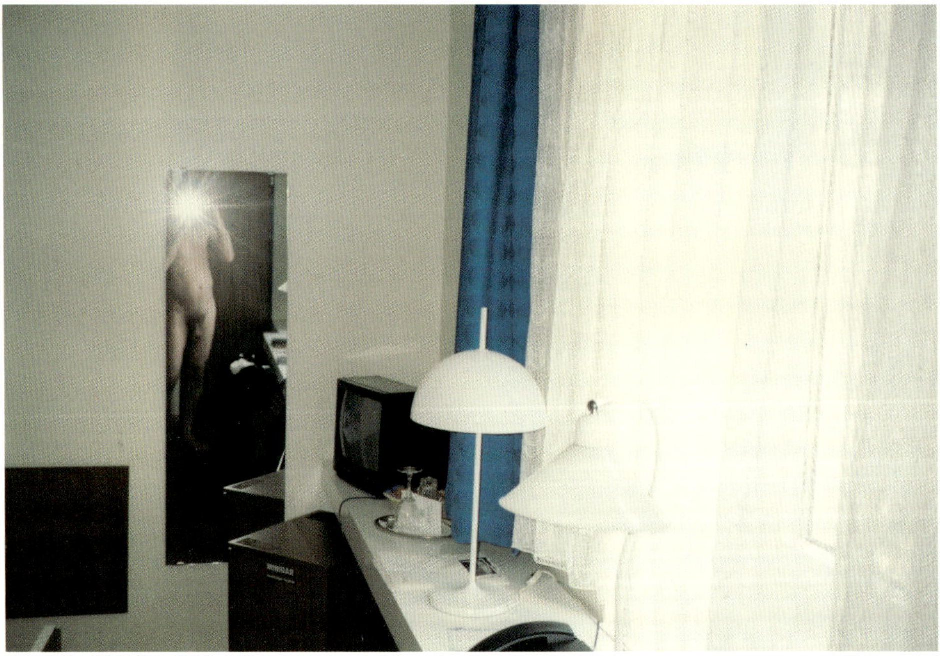

April 15, 2001, 10:00 am

I dreamed that my feminine self was appearing on a TV talk show. She was received enthusiastically, with the entrance of a heroine. From the hips down she had no body, but had been grafted onto a unicycle. She sat, withdrawn, on the verge of tears, hands folded in her lap, because she knew she was not a heroine, only one who had suffered loss.

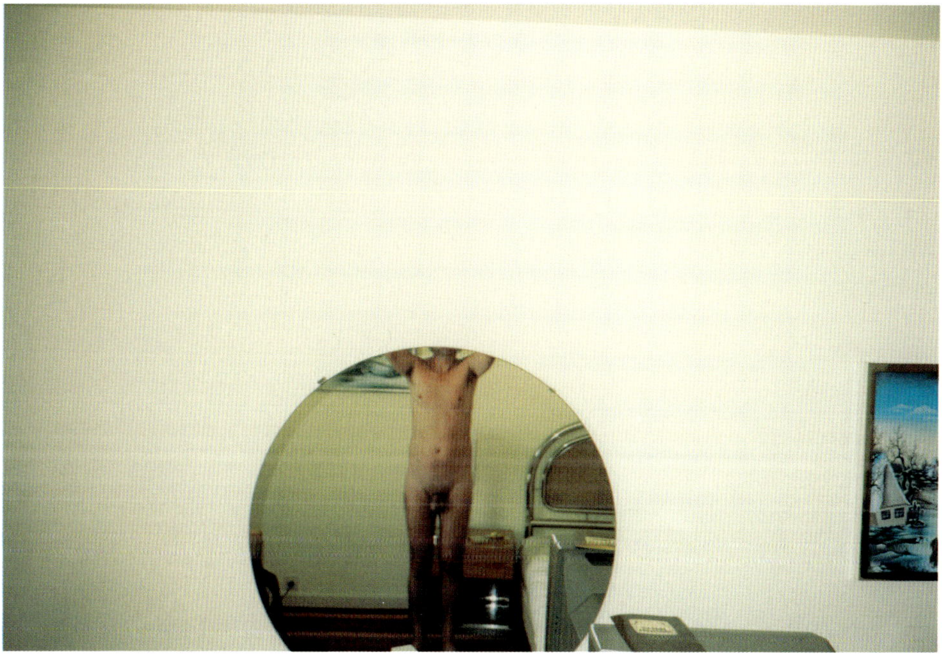

from **Mirror Photos**, 2000
color C-print
11 x 14 inches

August 27, 2001, 4:00 am

I dream that I am leaving. My friend Fern will be in charge of my swimming pool, which is bright turquoise. It seems that it is used by the public for some specific healing purpose. I am discussing the details of this with her. The dream was deeply unsettling. I felt it to be a premonition of death. But reading it again, as this book is going to press, I come to understand that it is about leaving the past behind.

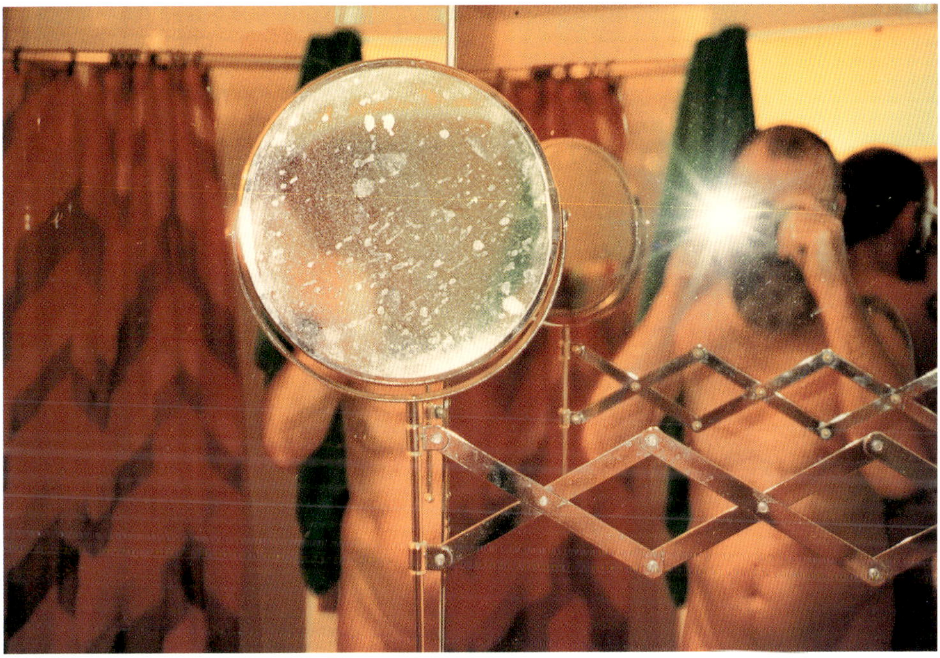

Mirror Mirror, 2002
wall drawing
dimensions variable

ne

of life;

be,

you are —

An acquaintance died in 1986, the first I knew to go: he left behind a book by Erwin Panofsky called *Tomb Sculpture*, which gravitated to my apartment. It was only after I had lived through many more deaths, including those of my two partners, that I came to look at it in detail. I kept it all those years because I knew it was somehow intended for me, but in what way I was not aware.

When I began working on my self-portrait *AA, August 22, 2000*, I read Panofsky's history of the representation of death. The phenomenon of the *transi* called out to me: despite often macabre effects, these images of the dead, usually naked and partially decomposed, picture the "collective relevance" of life on earth, rather than individual achievements and status. They were common in northern Europe in the fifteenth and sixteenth centuries.

An example is the tomb slab of Johannes Gmainer (died 1482), a mayor in Lower Bavaria, shown as "an almost skeletonized cadaver, violently attacked by vermin...and addressing the beholder as follows: 'Sum speculum vitae, Johannes Gmainer, at rite/Tales vos eritis, fueram quandoque quod estis' ('In me behold the looking glass of life:/Such you will be, for I was what you are')."

Tomb slab of Johannes Gmainer (died 1482)
red marble
St. Jakob, Straubing, Germany
from: Erwin Panofsky, *Tomb Sculpture*, (New York, Abrams, undated.)

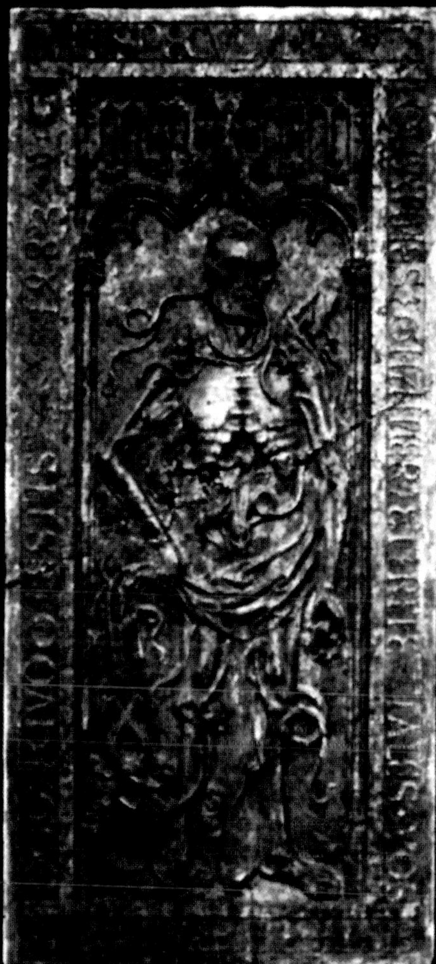

During my first year of Architecture School I volunteered for the Psychology Department's experiments in sensory deprivation. I agreed to be locked in a padded coffin for a week, in exchange for a sum of money, which I badly needed.

When I arrived, in the loose-fitting clothes they requested, they gave me a battery of tests, and then led me to a large room, padded on all four walls. I think it might have been an old classroom, but there were no windows. In the middle of the room was a long padded box, raised off the ground so that no vibration could reach the occupant. I was blindfolded, and my ears were padded. I lay down in the box with a button close to my hand in case I needed help. The box was closed on top of me and I was left in a sort of soft, sultry darkness, which was without dimension. Three times a day I was briefly removed from the box to use the bathroom and eat a sandwich, but for the most part I was left to think, and then to dream. Time disappeared. I had no consciousness of day or night, and images came and went: reality, thought and dreams, the conscious and the unconscious, all merged in a sort of continuous flow. Whenever I was let out of the box, I found myself intensely aware of physical space, although I remained blindfolded. I knew exactly the location of the walls and the dimensions of the spaces I passed through.

After three days I began to panic, and pushed the button. I wanted to end the experiment. It was Saturday, the day of the Santa Claus parade, and the woman who gave the tests was at the parade with her son. They asked if I could hold out until they located her, and they sounded so plaintive that I agreed. Three hours later she appeared, let me out of the box, gave me my tests, and I went home. The colors of nature were intense and sublime, the trunks of the trees shaggy with damp bark: my vision seemed precise and perfect.

I knew then that I belonged in that perfect box, that I would return to it.

AA Bronson, August 22, 2000 (detail), 2000
photograph by Arne Svenson

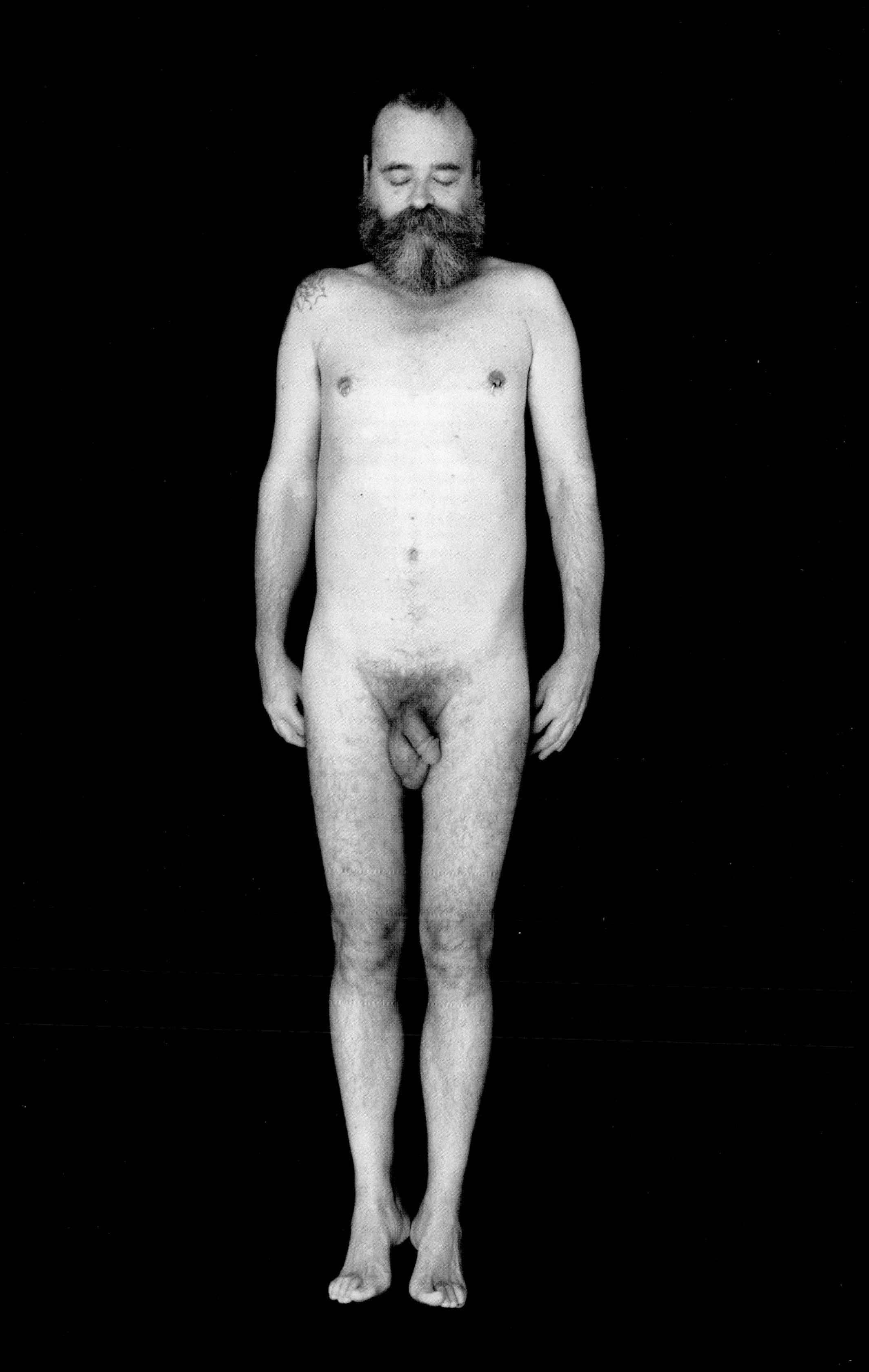

In third year university, at the age of twenty years, I had what I describe as an extended nervous breakdown. I was living at the time with two friends, Ralph and Paul, in the top of an old house. We were in the third floor garret, and the three of us shared a one-bedroom apartment.

I am thinking of the morning that I opened a little trap door into the eaves of the house and crawled in. I closed the door behind me and lay there in the dark for the rest of the day, listening to the sounds of the house, the occasional movement carried upwards from the first floor, and the faint creaking of the old house itself. By the late afternoon, Paul and Ralph had returned and I was conscious of their conversation. Their faint curiosity as to my whereabouts turned to worry and then to mild panic. At some point they decided that I had never left the house, and then there were the sounds of the search, under the bed, in the closets. Finally the little door by my face opened, letting in light, and Paul dragged me out. That's all I remember.

AA Bronson, August 22, 2000, 2000
ebonized wood, plexiglas and silver gelatin print
79-1/2 x 28-3/8 x 19-5/8 inches
installation view at Wien Secession, Vienna, Austria
photo: Margherita Spiluttini

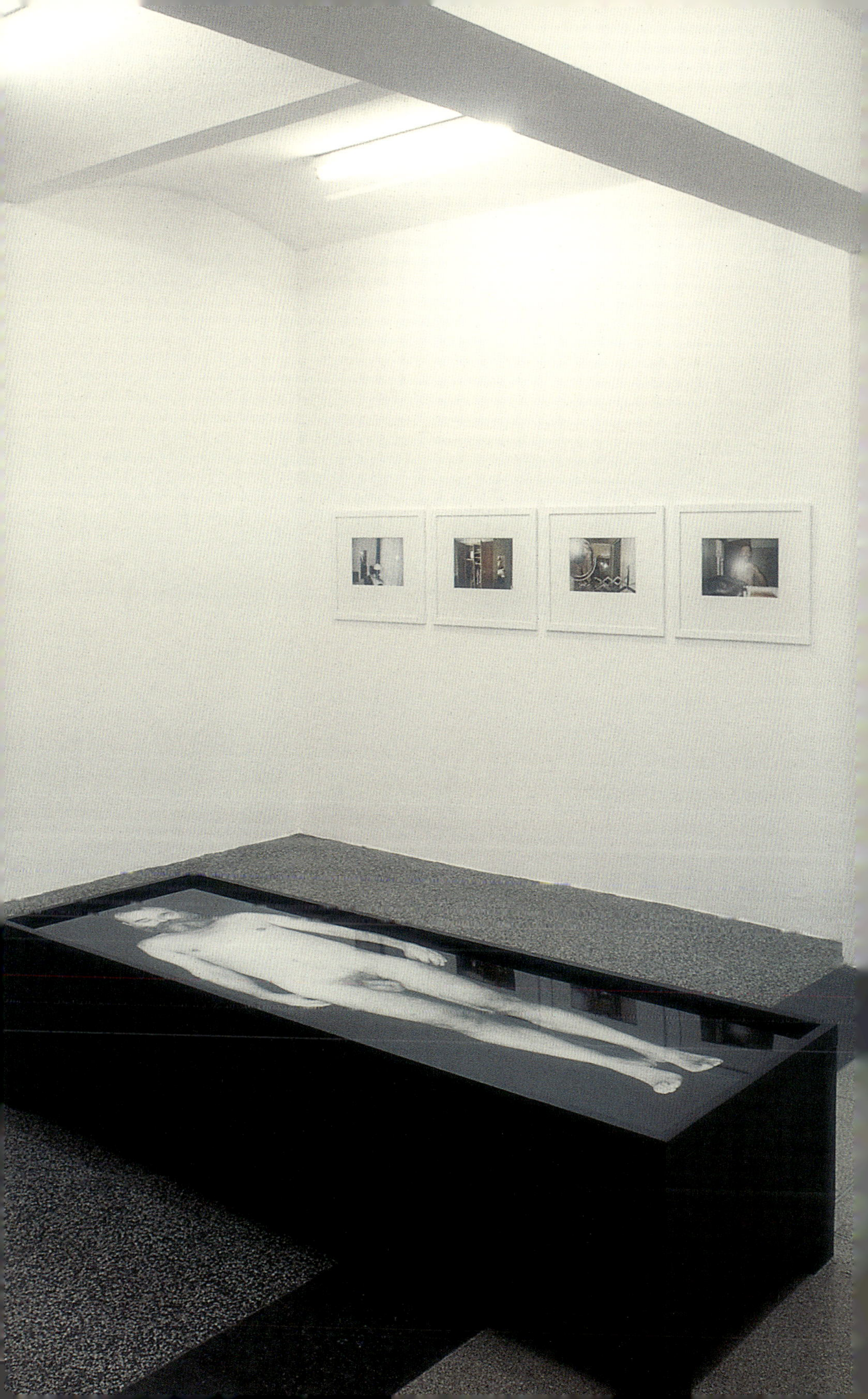

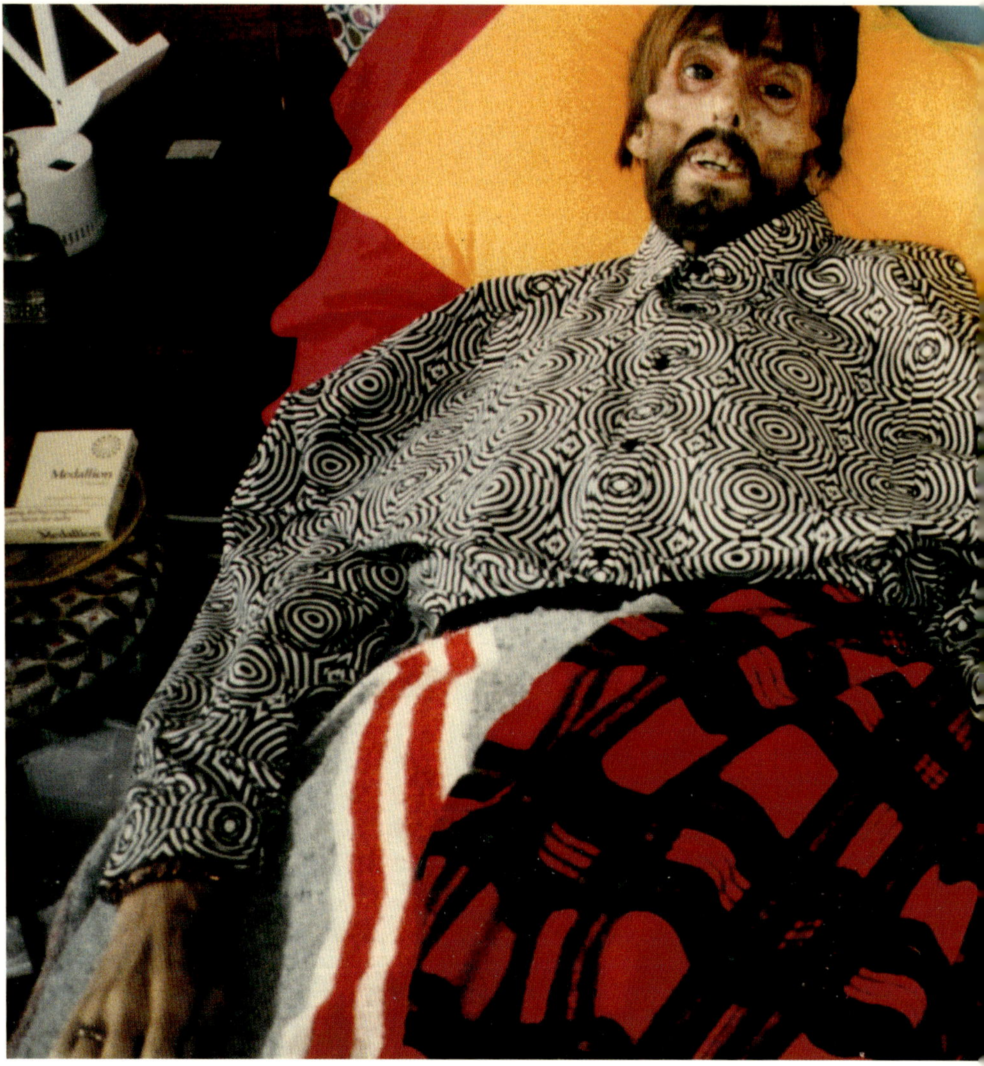

Felix, June 5th, 1994, 1994-99
lacquer on vinyl
120 x 240 inches

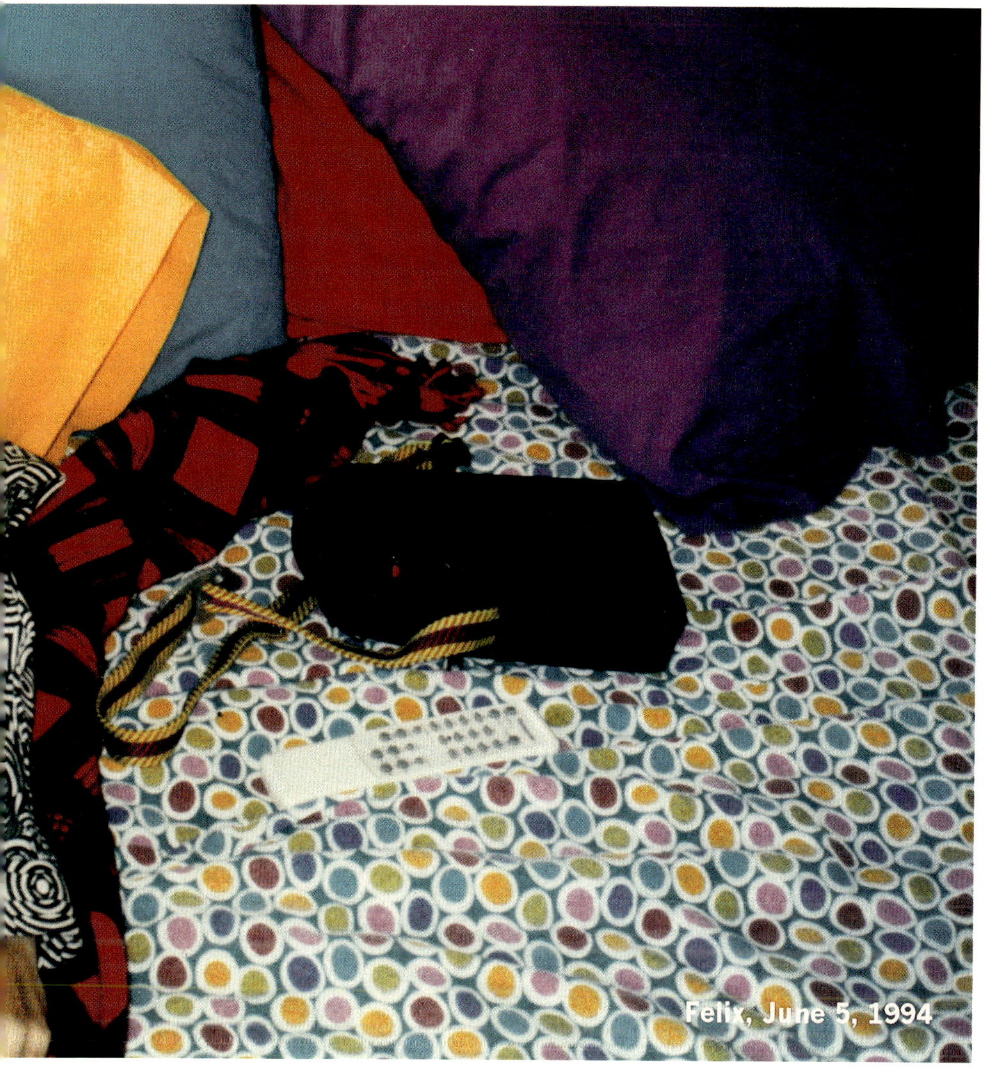

Felix, June 5, 1994

I made the photograph of Felix, which you see on the preceding pages, a few hours after his death. He is arranged to receive visitors, and his favorite objects are gathered about him: his television remote control, his tape-recorder, and his cigarettes. Felix suffered from extreme wasting, and at the time of his death his eyes could not be closed: there was not enough flesh left on the bone.

Felix and Jorge and I lived and worked together from 1969 until 1994. This communal life ended when Jorge died of AIDS on February 3, 1994. Felix followed shortly after, on June 5, 1994.

These bodies are our houses. We live in them as temporary tenants for a few years, for this short lifetime. We inhabit physical structures which mimic our physical form: windows to see, temperature controls, waste disposal systems. We gather these houses in towns and cities. By day we live in these cities as if they were permanent, relatively unchanging, while at night we inhabit the continuous flux of the dream world without questioning its fluidity.

But in fact both are dream worlds, both equally fluid: we might wake up at any time from one and find ourselves in the other.

Felix and Jorge and I lived and worked together for twenty-five years: during that time we became one organism, one group mind, one nervous system; one set of habits, mannerisms and preferences. We presented ourselves as a 'group' called General Idea and we pictured ourselves in doctored photographs as the ultimate artwork of our own design: we transformed our borrowed bodies into props, significations manipulated to create an image, a reality. We chose to inhabit the world of mass media and advertising. We made of ourselves the artists we wanted to be.

Since Jorge and Felix died, I have been struggling to find the limits of my own body as an independent organism, as a being outside of General Idea. Over the last five years I have found myself, much like a stroke victim, learning again the limits of my nervous system, how to function without my extended body (no longer three heads, twelve limbs), how to create possibilities from my reduced physicality.

I have had to place Jorge and Felix and General Idea at a distance. This has been difficult, like escaping from my own skin.

Dear Felix, by the act of exhibiting this image in this exhibition I declare that we are no longer of one mind, one body. I return you to General Idea's world of mass media, there to function without me.

We need to remember that the diseased, the disabled and, yes, even the dead walk among us. They are part of our community, our history, our continuity. They are our co-inhabitants in this dream city.

Untitled (for General Idea), 1997
set of three white Bertoia side chairs with red/green/blue vinyl cushions
Edition of 9 plus 2 APs
29 x 19 x 22 inches each chair
published by 1301 PE projects and editions, Los Angeles

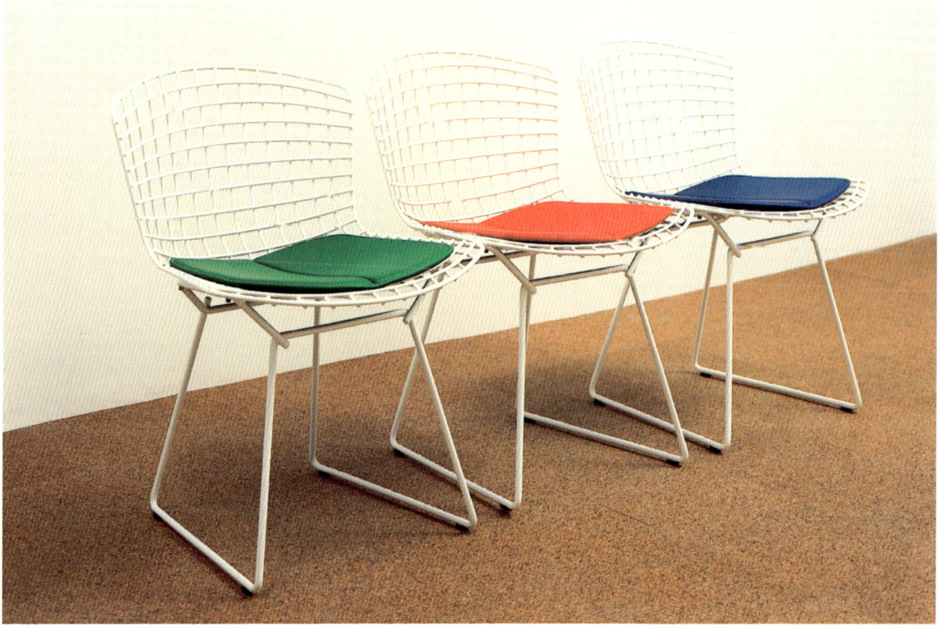

A page from my notebook:

June 14th, 1999 4 a.m.

A dream, crystal clear, in which I was saying goodbye to Jorge and Felix, from which I awoke with the sound of deep sobbing (in my dream). First Felix—we told each other what a great time we'd had together. Then he left and I was looking through some things, a silk-screened tablecloth we had hoped to transform into a multiple, with text, and I wondered if I would ever do it. I folded it carefully and put it back in its box. Then Jorge arrived. He had his lips pursed and was wearing a sort of silvery magenta lipstick, startlingly bright. I said how did he do it, and he said he had matched the color when we were last together earlier. The color had some significance. Did it match something I was wearing? He called it "azzuro." We were saying goodbye when I was awoken by the sound of deep sobbing, coming from a deeper level, bubbling up from beneath the dream, from a deeper self.

I should silk-screen the description of this dream onto a tablecloth.

Felix and Jorge, June 14th 1999, 1999
serigraph on linen
edition of 12 plus 3 APs
65 1/2 x 56 1/4 inches

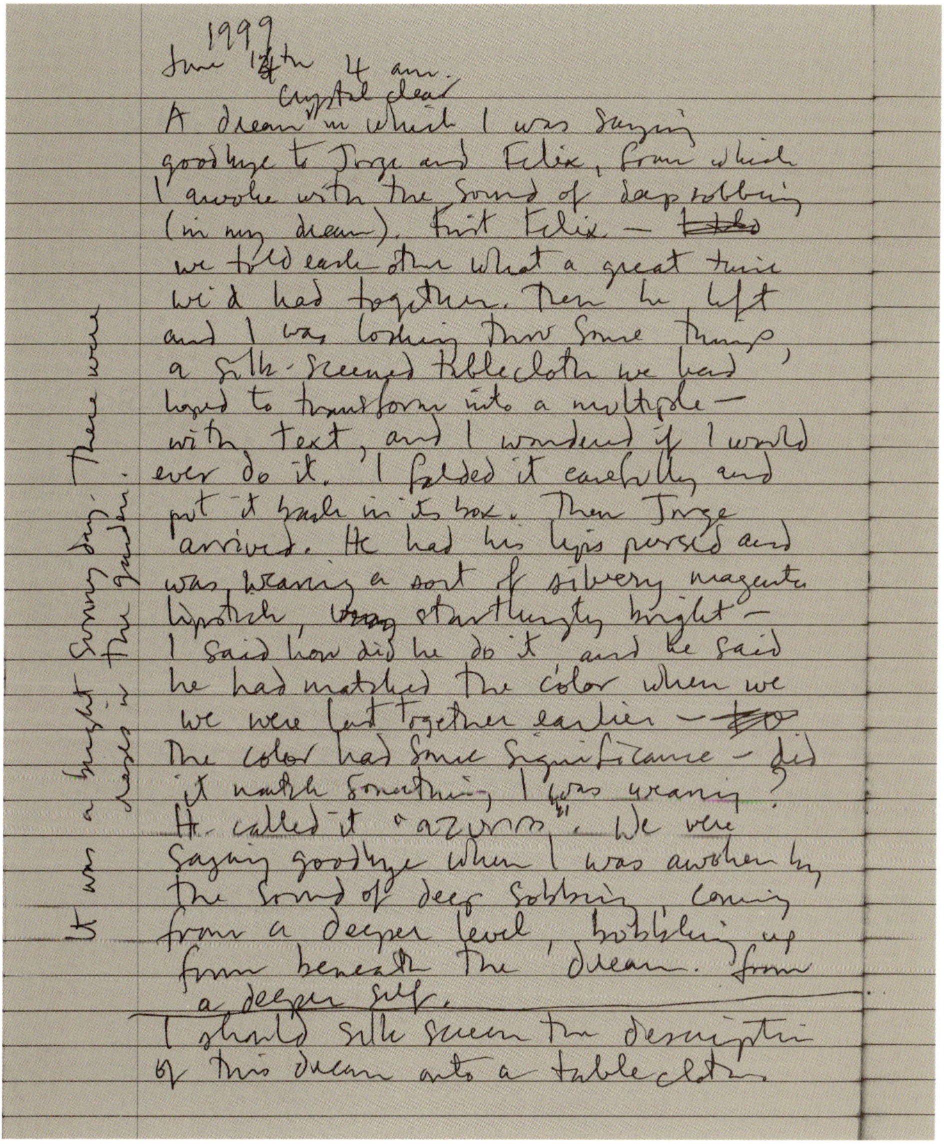

June 14th 1999 4 am.

A dream "crystal clear" in which I was saying goodbye to Jorge and Felix, from which I awoke with the sound of deep sobbing (in my dream). First Felix — we told each other what a great time we'd had together. Then he left and I was looking thru some things, a silk-screened tablecloth we had hoped to transform into a multiple — with text, and I wondered if I would ever do it. I folded it carefully and put it back in its box. Then Jorge arrived. He had his lips pursed and was wearing a sort of silvery magenta lipstick, startlingly bright — I said how did he do it and he said he had matched the color when we we were last together earlier — The color had some significance — did it match something I was wearing? He called it "azurro". We were saying goodbye when I was awoken by the sound of deep sobbing coming from a deeper level, bubbling up from beneath the 'dream.' from a deeper self.

I should silk screen the description of this dream onto a tablecloth.

It was a bright sunny day. There were roses in the garden.

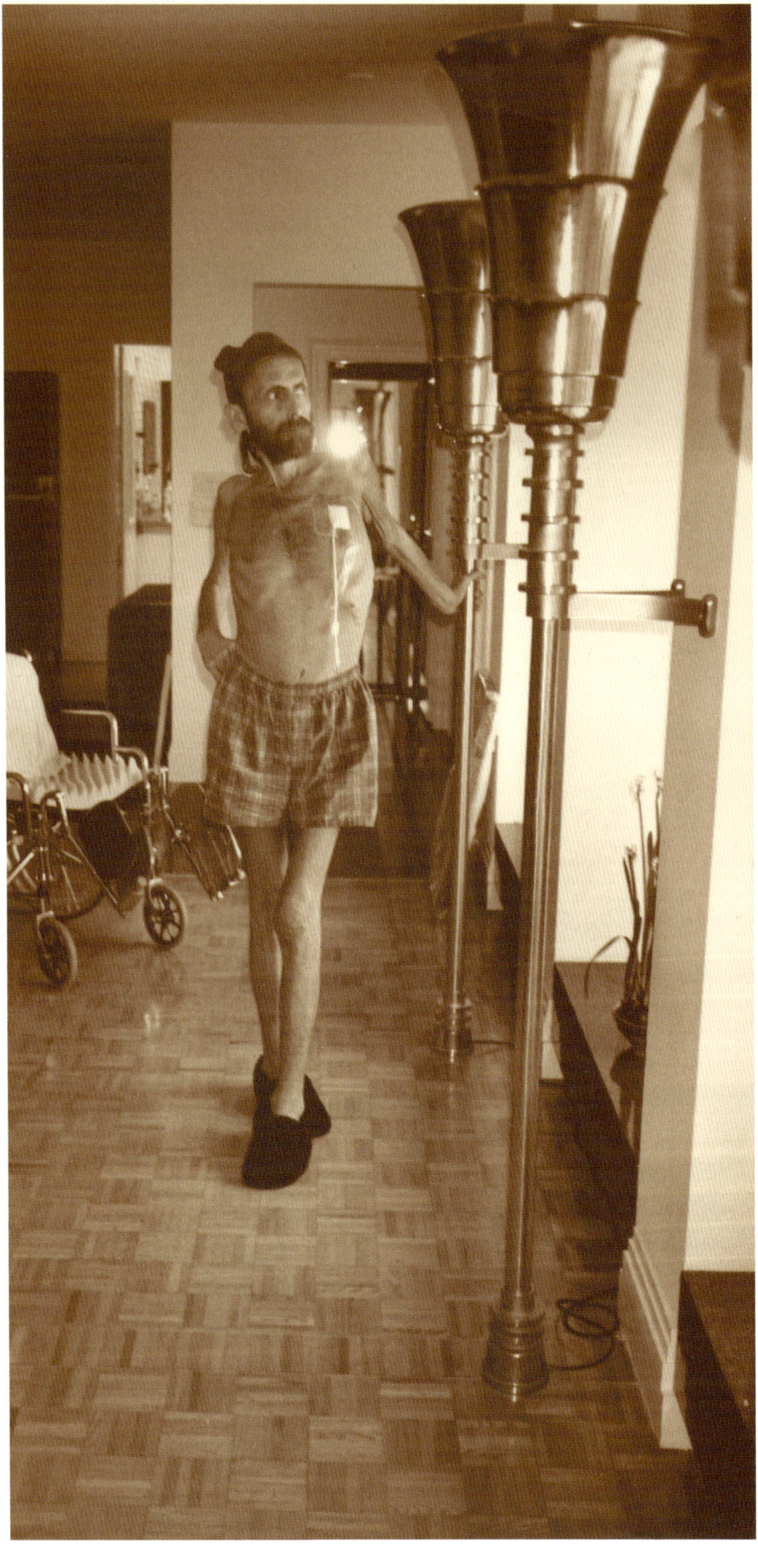

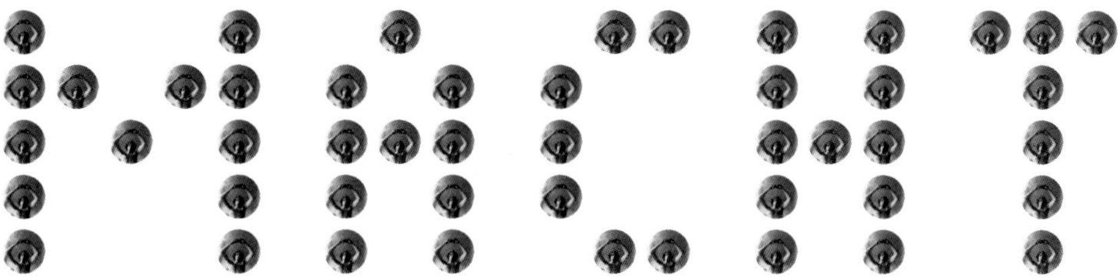

Arbeit Macht Frei, 2000
8" diameter convex circular plastic mirrors
approximately 5 by 45 feet installed
installation view at Ursula Blickle Stiftung, Unterowisheim, Germany
(work by Nayland Blake in foreground) photograph by Wolfgang Günzel

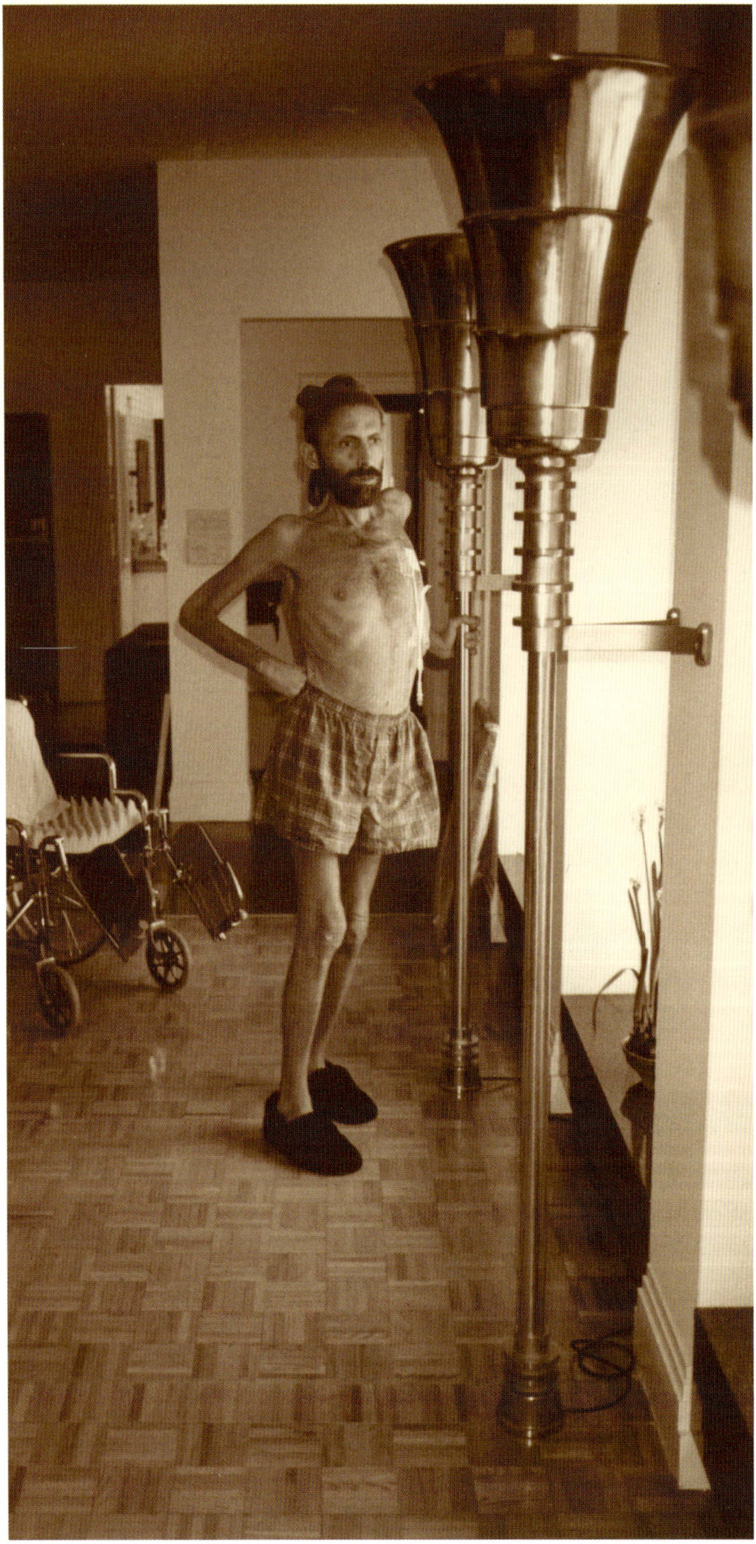

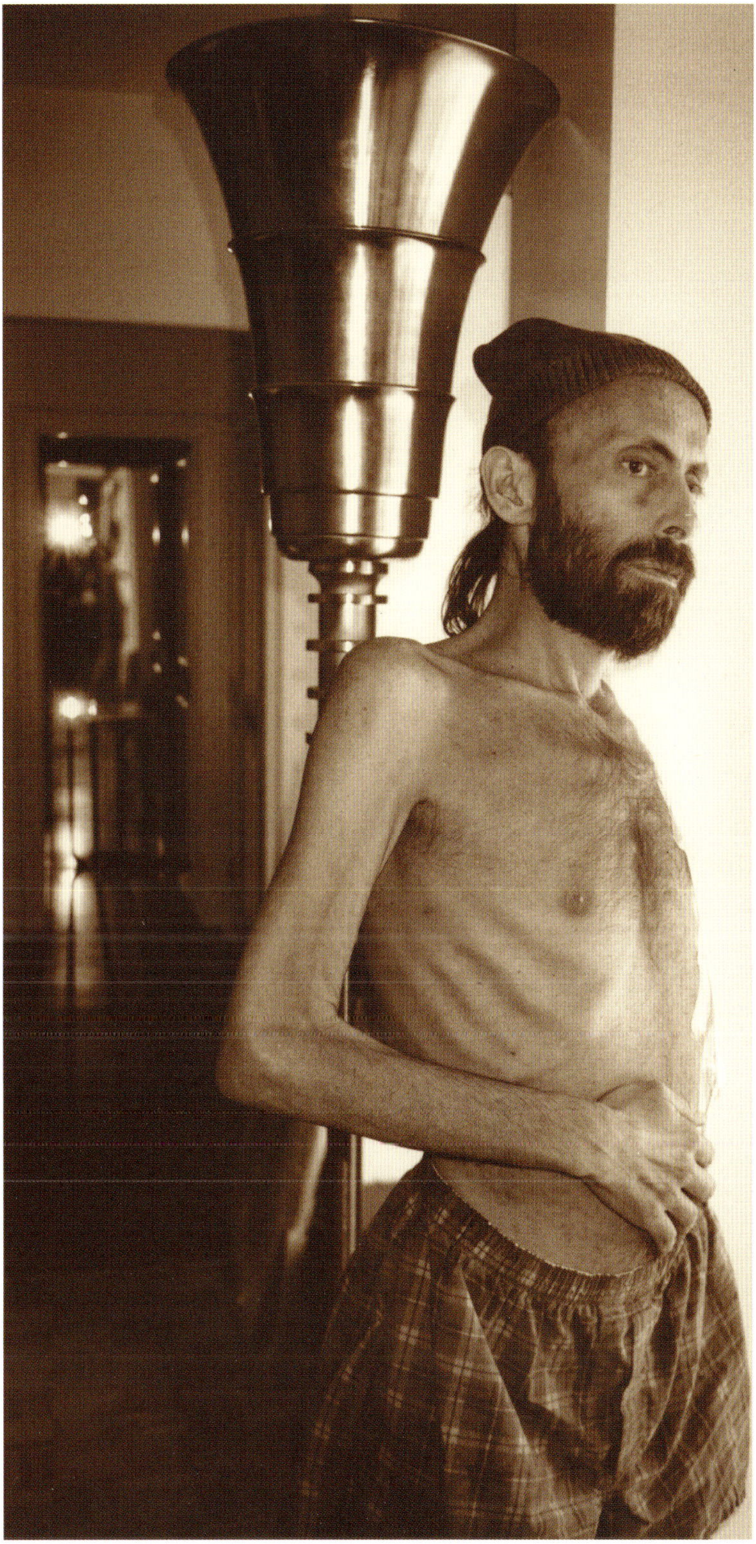

About a week before Jorge died, he asked me to take these photographs.

Jorge's father had been a survivor of Auschwitz, and he had the idea that he looked exactly as his father had on the day of his release. He wanted to document that similarity, that family similarity of genetics and of disaster. It has occurred to me since that the moments in history are rare when entire communities are erased, leaving surrounding communities intact. The gay community suffered ongoing losses through the late eighties and most of the nineties; the Jewish community suffered similarly during the Holocaust. I have friends who can count over fifty friends and acquaintances lost to AIDS over a fifteen year period. Under these circumstances, the concepts of grieving and Traumatic Stress Syndrome become meaningless: grief and trauma are buried in the ongoing onslaught of wasting and death, the continuous interweaving of care-taking, funerals, memorials, anniversaries, and more deaths.

Jorge was blind when I took these photos. I had to act as his mirror in order that he could look 'normal'. "Should my eyes be like this?" he asked. "A little more open," I replied, "No, not quite that much."

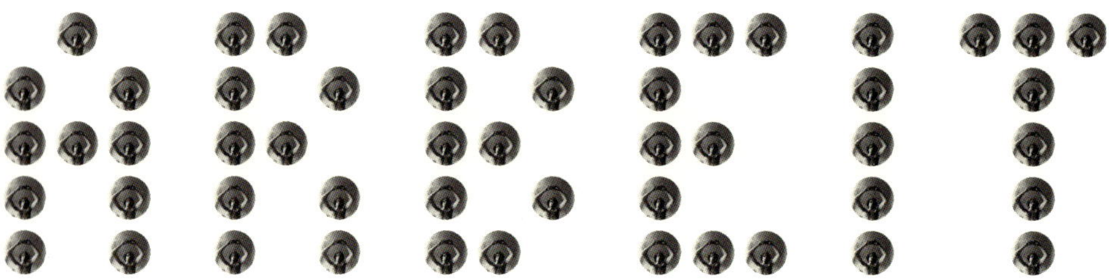

<

Jorge, February 3, 1994, 1994-2000
sepia on mylar, edition of 3
three parts, 72-1/2 x 36-1/4 inches each

I have been thinking about group trauma, the sort of repeated and ongoing trauma that leaves whole communities devastated, decimated, such as the AIDS pandemic, or the Holocaust. In particular, I have been reading about Auschwitz. I have been wading through the data presented in Auschwitz 1940-1945, five volumes of documentation published by the Auschwitz-Birkenau State Musuem. I have immersed myself in this swamp of detail, wanting to address Auschwitz, and all that it stands for, without knowing how I could do so, or how I could bring it into the present, into the presence of my own life and times. One morning I awoke with a vision complete in my mind: digital lettering, each letter the size of my own body, each pixel made of a circular mirror, and spelling out the slogan: ARBEIT MACHT FREI. The mirrors are from my youth, the convex mirrors with which I constructed my earliest self-portraits. The slogan is that on the portal to Auschwitz, the slogan with which each inmate was greeted; it also captures the Protestant and North American work ethic: "work will set you free." In my mind's eye, the mirrors are not lit; rather, the spectators are lit. The spectator becomes the ultimate subject: the piece is quite literally a reflection on the viewer.

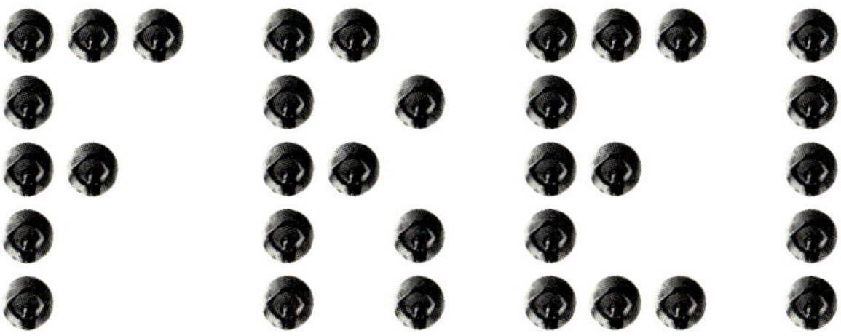

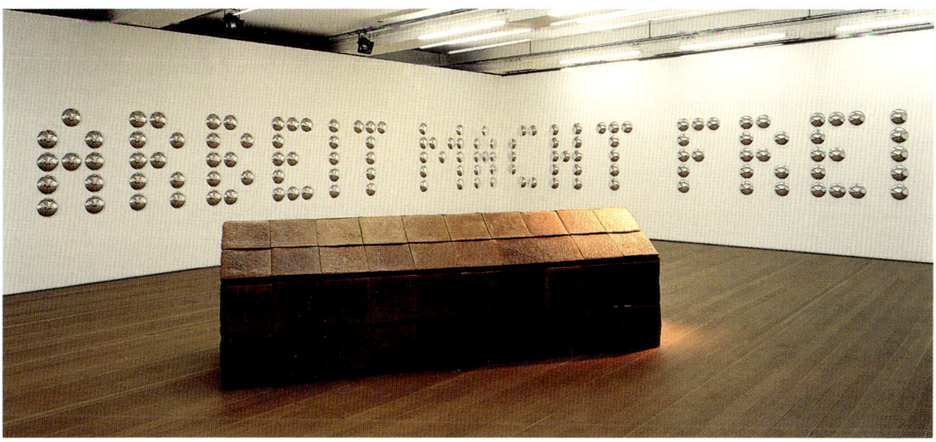

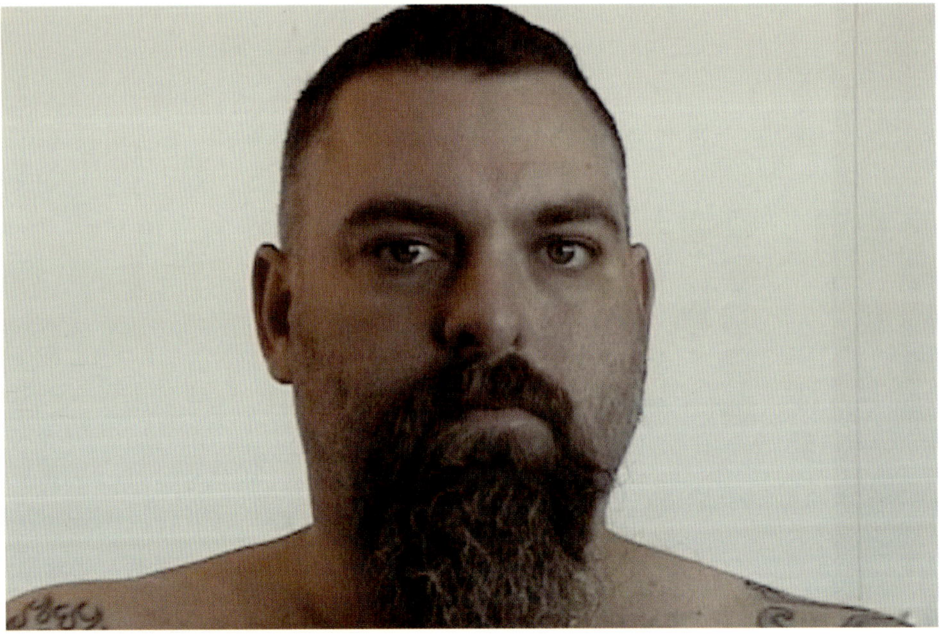

Nayland and AA, June 20, 2001 (Coat), 2001
3-channel video collaboration with Nayland Blake
3 DVDs, 7 minutes each; projection with two monitors

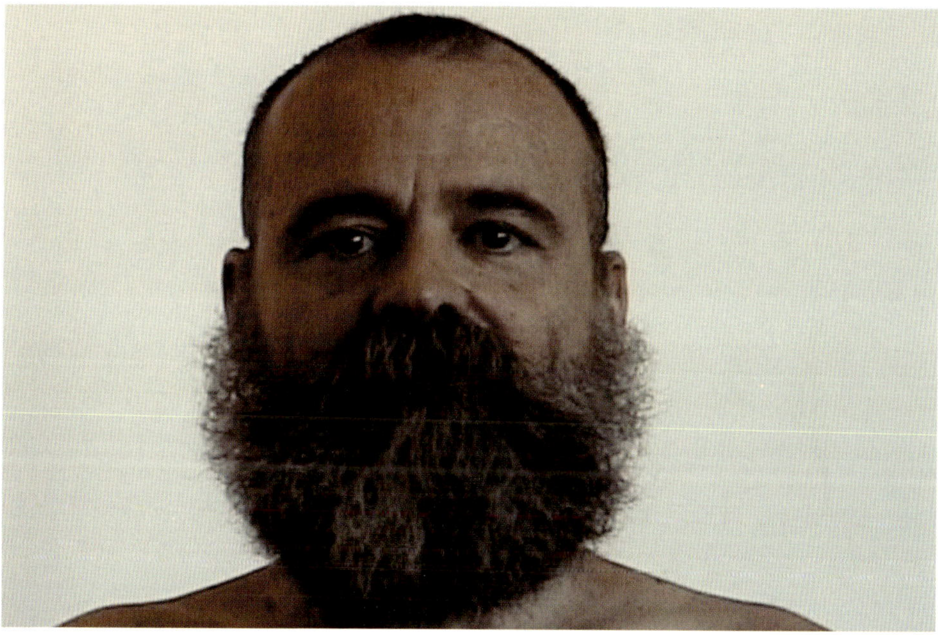

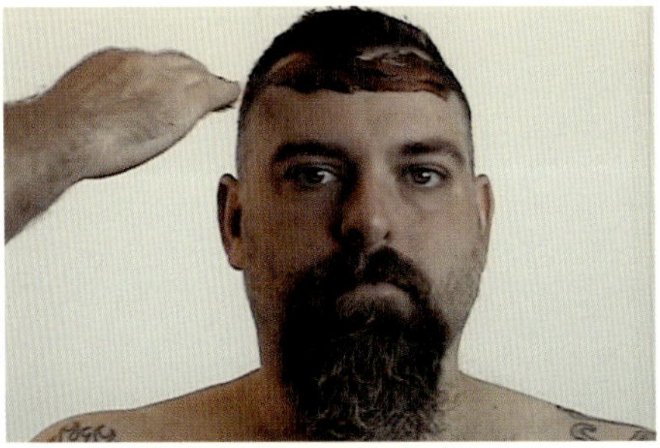
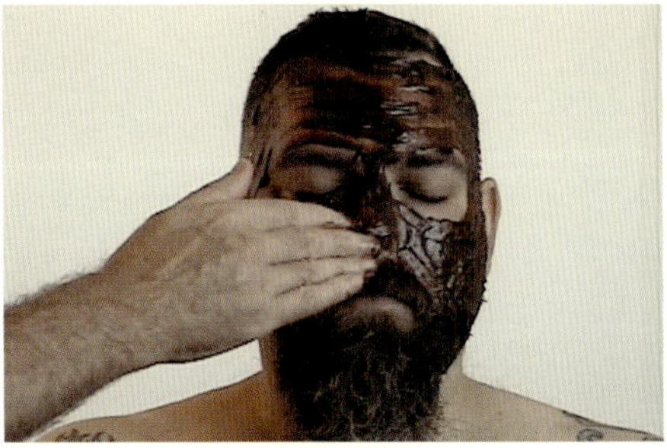
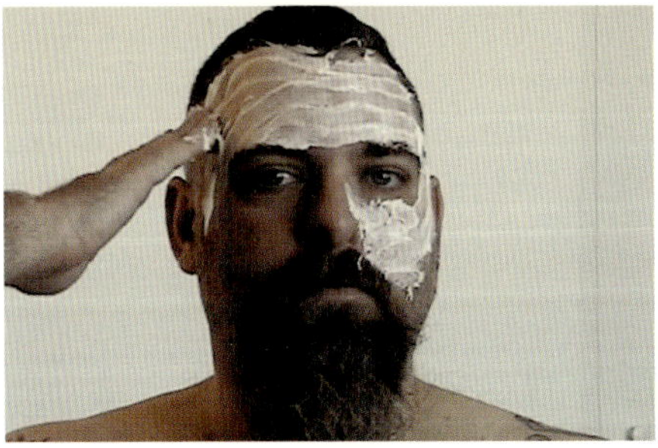
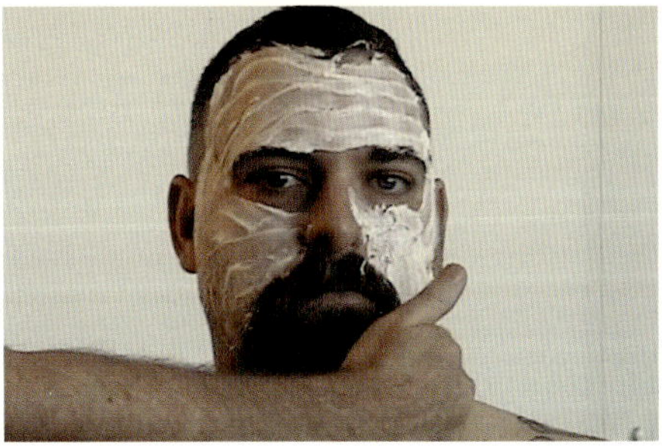

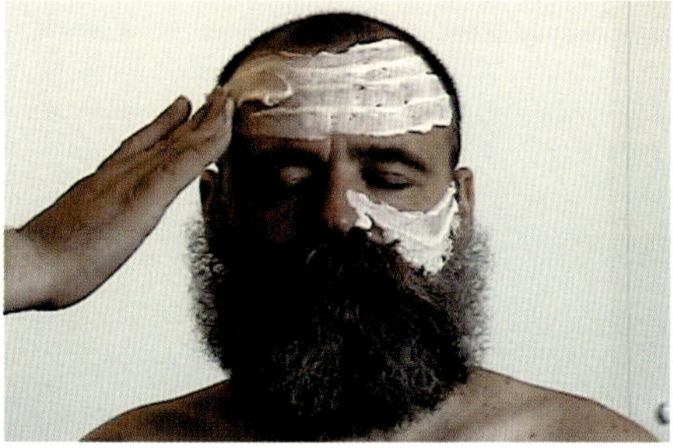
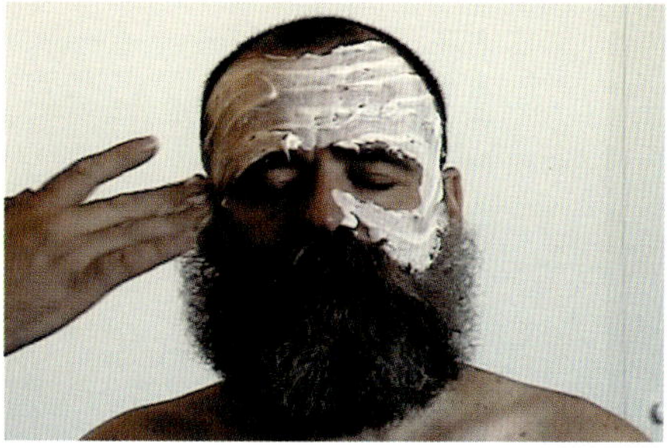
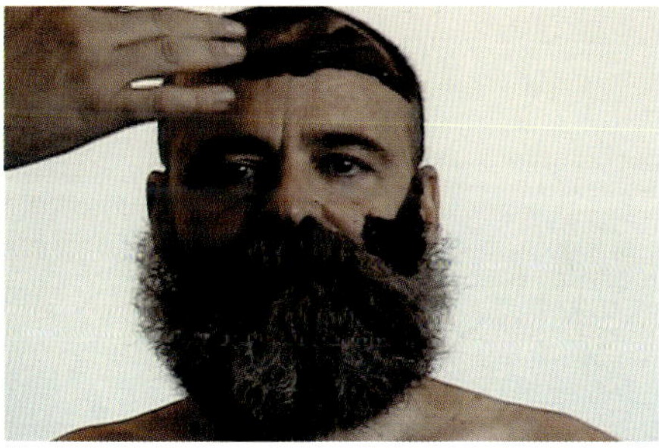
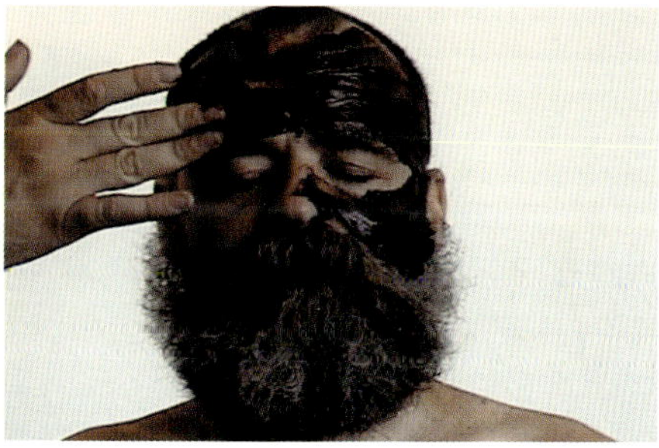

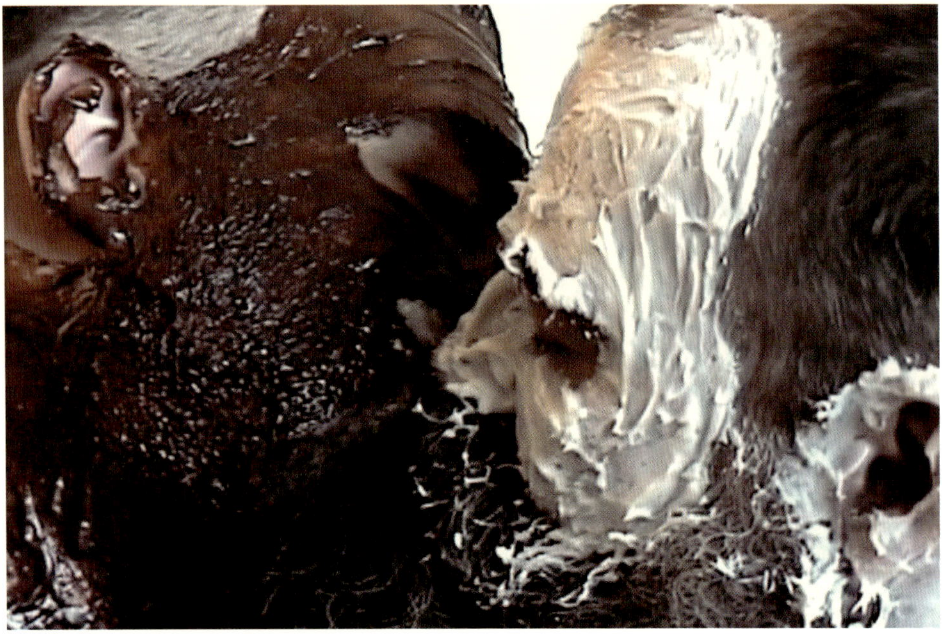

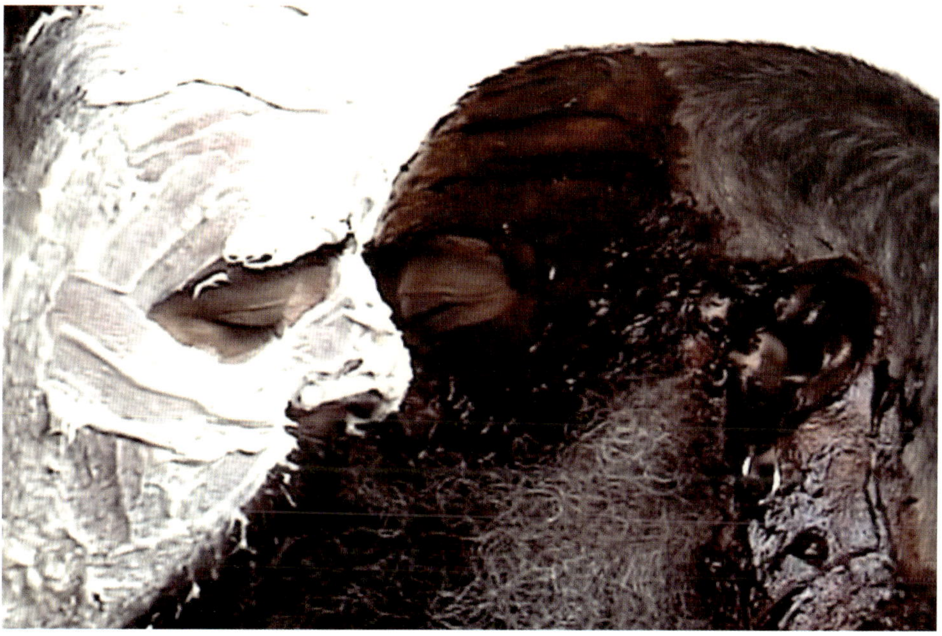

January 23, 2002

Dear Nayland,

I am writing this text to tell you how much it meant to me to make this video together.
I am 55 years old, you are 41. In a way, a very simplistic way, we mirror each other: big beards, tattooed, gay, visual artists. Our practices have mirrored each other too: an eclectic mix of media and methods, from sculpture and installation to performance and video, and an ongoing awareness of political, social and sexual issues.
I came to this collaboration as I feel an older gay man must in coming to a younger, as a willing mirror and as an acknowledgement of the other man's essential being.
As gay men, we have too little acknowledgement in this world. We must bear witness for each other, and we do.
"The Kiss" is a universal theme: the kiss of life, and the kiss of death.
We are each all too practiced at being "the other". I think we are both "survivors" although we have not talked about surviving. We talked about our childhood; about race, gender, sexual preference; about food, intimacy and trust. We talked about the process of making this video.
The video is almost obsessively symmetrical. I apply brown, then white, to you (Betty Crocker canned frosting, but that's another story); you apply white, then brown, to me. We kiss: brown on white, then white on brown. The symmetrics of the system were important to us both, and I think we solved them.
The performance of the kiss itself: this had to be an act of total intimacy and total trust, because it functioned as the sealing point of the piece ("sealed with a kiss"); and because it had to function outside of our personal relationships. We kissed with our hands at our sides, a most unnatural position, rather than clasping each other, as might be expected. And yet this kiss was tender and giving: I experienced it as I experienced the entire project, slightly distanced, and yet intimate; I could call it a reflective kiss.
I suppose that this piece is about a balance of power. Throughout the entire piece, I let you take the lead. I considered it appropriate in my position as the older man. I wanted to embed myself in your process, rather than impose my process on you. I hope I was successful in that. And I think that approach is reflected in the symmetry of power that the video relates: it is the story of our relationship, or what our relationship becomes through the making of this work.
As I write this, I pause to consider if there is anything else that I want to say: I want to thank you. I want to thank you for the trust you placed in me and I hope I returned that trust in kind. We seemed to proceed in a perfect unison, such a rare experience in collaboration, and I thank you for that, too. Finally, I thank you for the essential experience of loving trust and intimacy, even tenderness, that suffused the entire experience, and which I find so central to how I want to live my life and art today.

Sincerely Yours,

AA Bronson

January 25, 2002

AA -

I remember how tenative our early conversations were about this project. I did feel that same stage fright that I felt the first time I went out with an older man. And then again I flashed back to our earlier encounters: in San Francisco at your show at Artspace, or in Baltimore where you gave me advice on an altar I had built in the middle of the museum. I was anxious about us working together but felt we had a pretty good chance of getting some place interesting. I didn't think it would get so deep. Any collaboration is a dance. As we started I was really struck by your openess and good will and then as we watched the first tapes I saw us pass through a variety of roles as we got coated: clown, shaman, black-face performer, tarred and feathered, muddy Woodstock attendee, ghoul. I knew it was going to be all right.
One day after working a while we had a conversation looking out at the remains of the Christopher Street piers. You told me how you had first been brought there by Ray Johnson to see the all the art tucked away in the buildings as well as the all the men cruising, lounging. There is something here about mentorship and initiation. Our ages aren't all that different, but in a very real way we face each other across a generational divide: a divide in artistic generations, and in generations of artmaking. Like our kiss, our piece was a bridge across those divides. Thank you for that.

Nayland

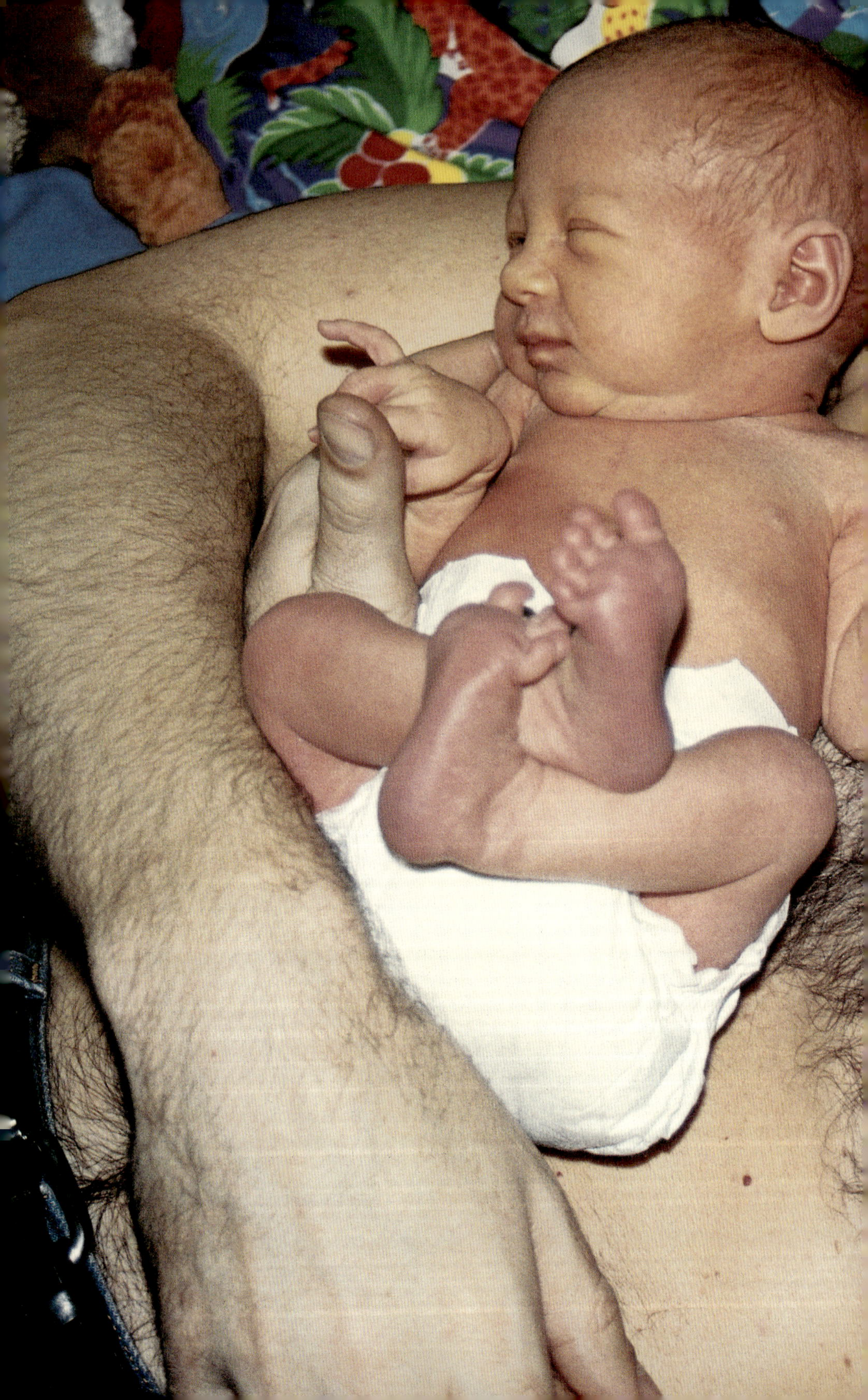

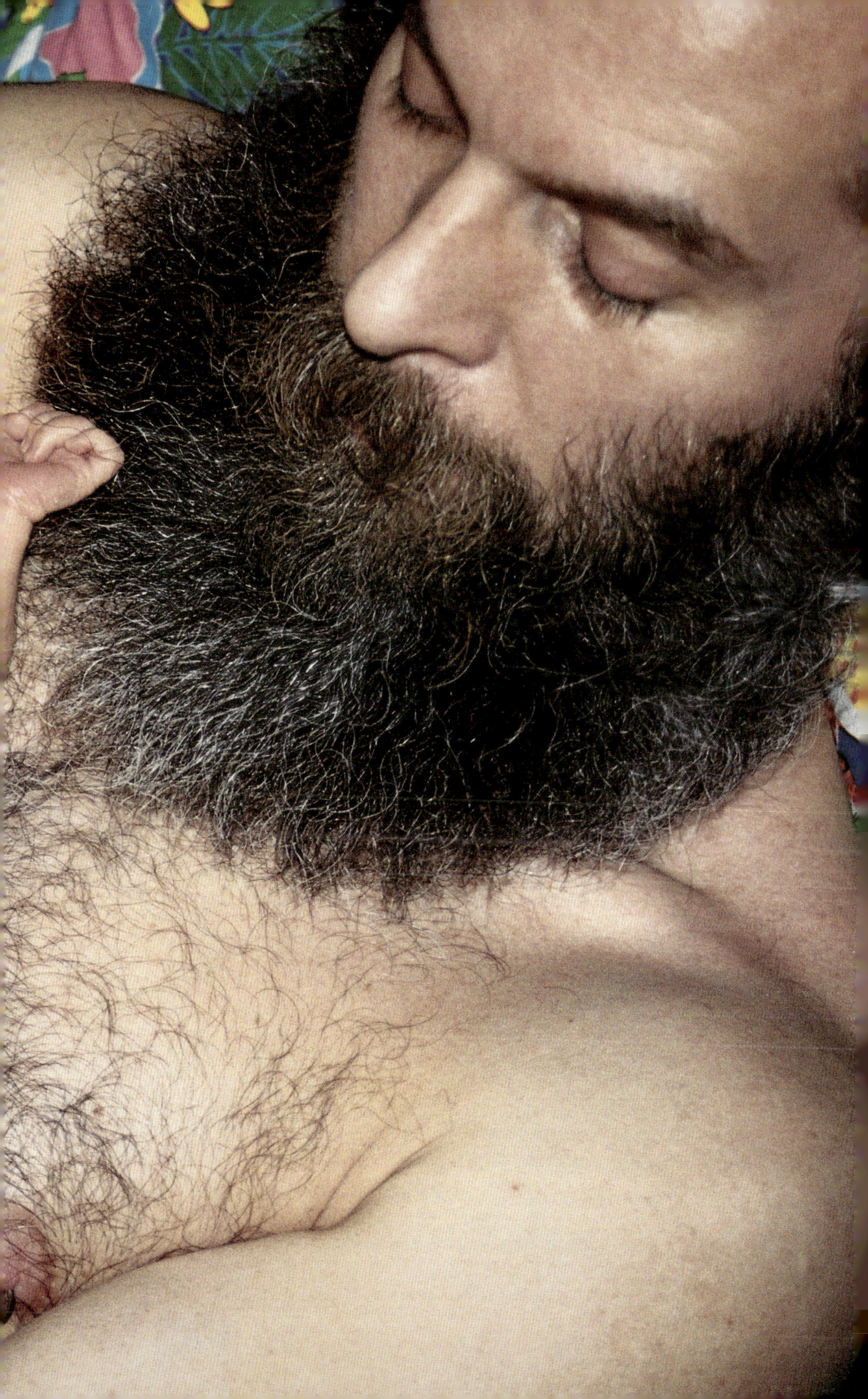

Anna was born on January 23, 2001, ten days before this picture was taken. Mark—her father, my spouse—is holding her here for the first time, and I am recording the encounter. She weighs five pounds, and she is cherry red, still raw from the difficulty of a breach birth, one month premature.

How to covey this labor of love, not the love of parent for parent, but the outpouring of love from two men, two women, towards the creation of this little being? Each of us knows the importance of love, the essential nature of unconditional love, and each of us participates in creating this movement, this flow of outwardly directed love which has created this child and which we will to carry her along in her journey through life and living.

< **Anna and Mark, February 3, 2001**, 2001-02
lacquer on vinyl
edition of 3 plus 1 AP
84 x 120 inches

Each of us – the child, the four parents, and you, the reader – is interdependent. Each of us is loving and loving another, and each of us is yearning towards union, and each of us is dying, and each of us is being born, each of us is bearing anew, and each of us is a fragment carried along in this river of love we call life.

AA BRONSON

born Vancouver, June 16, 1946
lives and works in Toronto and New York

AA Bronson lived and worked as part of the artists' group General Idea from 1969 until the deaths of his two partners in 1994. The exhibitions and bibliography listed below concern exhibitions of AA Bronson's solo work since that time.

Solo Exhibitions

1999	1301PE, Los Angeles
2000	*AA Bronson 1969-2001*, Vienna Secession, Vienna
	AA Bronson, Ecart, Basel
2001	*Negative Thoughts*, Museum of Contemporary Art, Chicago
	The Copyright marks the border between public and private domains, The Balcony, Toronto
2002	*Mirror Mirror*, MIT List Visual Arts Center, Cambridge

Group Exhibitions

1998	*Brain Multiples*, Art Metropole, Toronto
1999	*Dream City*, Museum Villa Stuck, Munich
2000	*La Biennale de Montréal 2000*, CIAC, Montréal
2001	*Angst: Fear of Loss* (touring): Blickle Foundation, Karlsruhe;Kunsthalle Graz, Graz
2002	*Whitney Biennial*, Whitney Museum of American Art, New York

Bibliography

1999 Astrid Wege, "In der Glaskugel", *Texte zur Kunst*, Heft 34, June 1999, pp. 157-162
AA Bronson, "Afterthought", *Canadian Art*, Toronto, Summer, 1999
Matthias Schübler, "Dream City", *Das Münchner Kunstjournal*, Heft 8/1999
Heinz Schütz, "Dream City", *Kunstforum International*, Band 145, May/June 1999

2000 *AA Bronson 1969-2000* (solo exhibition catalogue), Vienna Secession, Vienna
Henriette Horny, "Bilder über Lieber", *Kurier*, Vienna, October 5, 2000
"Bronson seeks life after death", *Wiener Zeitung*, Vienna, 17-23 October, 2000
Doris Krumpl, "Der Abschied als Neubeginn", *Der Standard*, Vienna, October 21, 2000
Gabriele Schor, "Dort, wo das Leben endet", *Neue Züricher Zeitung*, Zurich, October 30, 2000
"Augen der Seele", *Neue Wochenschau*, Vienna, November 1, 2000
Antje Mayer, "Alptraum: AA Bronson erinnert an Jorge und Felix", *Kunstzeitung*, November 2000.
Molly Amoli K. Shinhat, "Past, Present & Future", *Ottawa Xpress*, Ottawa, November 30, 2000.
Tout le Temps/Every Time, La Biennale de Montréal, CIAC, Montréal

2001 AA Bronson, *Negative Thoughts* (artist book), Museum of Contemporary Art, Chicago
Anne Glusker, "Collective Memory", *Elle*, New York, January 2001
Dieter Buchhart, "AA Bronson", *Kunstforum*, Bd. 153, Januar-Marz 2001
Don Shewey, "Good Grief", *The Advocate*, Los Angeles, February 13, 2001
Michael Rooks, "Letting Go of General Idea", *Dialogue*, Chicago, January/February 2001
Daphne Gordon, "The Copyright Marks The Border Between The Public And Private Domains, corrugated plastic, 2000", *The Toronto Star*, Toronto, February 10, 2001
John Mays, "A Tale of Two Friends", *National Post*, Toronto, April 4, 2001
Achy Obejas, "Piercing Negative Thoughts forces a rethinking of AIDS crisis", *The Chicago Tribune*, April 23, 2001
Kathryn Rosenfeld, "Triple Self-Potrait Minus Two", *New Art Examiner*, Chicago, July-August, 2001 (cover story)
Nancy Princenthal, "Artist's Book Beat", *Art on Paper*, July-August 2001
Gerald Hannon, "Negative Thoughts", *Canadian Art*, Toronto, Fall 2001
Kate Taylor, "Why Gallery-going is an art form", *Globe & Mail*, Toronto, July 26, 2001
"Out 100", *Out*, New York, December 2001

2002 Judy Stoffman, "Canadian Artist Honoured", *The Toronto Star*, Toronto, January 3, 2002

MIT LIST VISUAL ARTS CENTER ADVISORY COMMITTEE 2001-2002
Kitty Glantz, Jenny Frutchy: Chairs
Ruth Bowman
Blake Brasher (MIT class of '01)
Alan Brody (MIT Associate Provost for the Arts)
Michael Coden
Jerome I. Friedman (MIT Institute Professor)
Marjory Jacobson
Henry Jenkins (MIT Associate Professor, Literature)
Dorothy Lavine
Leroy Lavine
Vera G. List
Boris Magasanik (MIT Professor Emeritus, Biology)
Marian Marill
Andrea Miller-Keller
Andrea Nasher
A.G. Rosen
Jeanne Stanton
Peter Temin (MIT Elisha Gray II Professor, Economics)
David Wallace (MIT Assistant Professor of Engineering)
Jeanne Wasserman
Krysztof Wodiczko (MIT Professor of Architecture)

MIT LIST VISUAL ARTS CENTER STAFF
Director: Jane Farver
Curator: Bill Arning
Curator: Kathleen Goncharov
Administrative Officer: David Freilach
Registrar: John Rexine
Gallery Manager: Tim Lloyd
Education/Outreach Coordinator: Hiroko Kikuchi
Administrative Assistant: Barbra Pine

Gallery Attendants:
Cree Bruins
Kristin Johnson
Jennifer Johnson
Bryce Kauffman
Kate Keeler
Jeremiah Foster

Interns:
Justine Ashbee
Zeina Assaf
Dorothy Deák
Christine Downing
Chennie Huang
Chuck Lewin
Michelle Mandeville
Virginia Moon
Yasu Nakamuri
Paul Parcellin
Almitra Stanley